Audio Access Included

JAZZ SOLOS for Guitar

by Les Wise

T0045078

To access audio visit:
www.halleonard.com/mylibrary

Enter Code
4224-8398-7680-4974

ISBN 978-0-634-01391-1

7777 W. BLUEMOUND RD. P.O. BOX 13819 MILWAUKEE, WI 53213

Visit Hal Leonard Online at
www.halleonard.com

Table of Contents

Introduction

Hello, and welcome to ProLicks *Jazz Solos for Guitar*. In this book, I'm going to walk you through six original guitar solos. Each one is based on classic lead (and rhythm) patterns used in jazz and is full of licks and ideas that you'll be able to use in your own playing. We'll cover a variety of styles and techniques—including arpeggios, scales, tension and resolution, blues forms, chord soloing, virtuoso-style fills, and more—giving you a solid foundation in playing and improvising jazz guitar.

Many of the styles and techniques in this book are based on the masterful soloing of players like Wes Montgomery, Joe Pass, Herb Ellis, Tal Farlow, George Benson, and more. You'll be able to listen to me solo using many of their favorite techniques, then I'll dissect each and every solo, note for note, so that you can master these styles as well.

How to Use This Book

As you work your way through the solos in this book, you'll discover that there are a lot of short phrases that you can learn, lift out, and use in your own style of playing. In other words, you don't have to learn each solo exactly the way it was played on the track. You can listen through the audio, hear everything that I'm going to play for you, then go back and pick out the phrases you like best. Then you can learn those phrases and incorporate them into your own style of playing. It's good practice to take all of these ideas and then mix them in with what you already know how to play.

Of course, there are things to be learned by playing an entire solo: how the solo builds, how to make a transition from one chorus to the next, how to begin and end the whole thing. Those are elements of style that make the phrases fit together so that they actually sound good. But the individual phrases themselves can be picked out and used in practically any jazz solo. With a little tweaking, these phrases can also be used in songs with different tempos and in different keys.

In addition to performing the six complete solos, I'm going to explain each one in depth, phrase by phrase. Each phrase will include Practice Points—detailed directions that will help you understand my note choices and give you ideas for coming up with your own solo phrases over the given chord progressions, using various tricks and techniques. Once you've listened to a solo, start learning it phrase by phrase using the Practice Points to help you.

When you get through, you'll know all the phrases and be able play them along with the solo track or with the rhythm-only track at the end of the chapter—a full-band, minus-guitar track that's also included with the ProLicks audio. Playing along with the rhythm-only tracks will give you an opportunity to get a feel for how your phrasing sounds against a rhythm section and whether or not you're playing correctly. Plus, you can use these tracks to improvise your own jazz solos.

Some of the phrases are easier than others. Some are slower; some are faster. Take your time. Practice each phrase as many times as you need to get it right. And most of all, have fun!

Tuning notes for reference can be found on track 16.

Before You Begin

The guitar sound in jazz is typically clean and warm, with a full-bodied tone and perhaps a touch of reverb. Set your amp clean, roll off the highs, and aim for a smooth, rich tone. The major jazz players almost all use hollowbody electric guitars, such as a Gibson ES-175, Guild Manhattan, or Gretsch White Falcon. But don't worry: If you don't have a hollowbody, you can still play jazz. Many modern jazz guitarists use solidbody guitars and sound just fine.

Also, traditional jazz players don't rely on bends as much as blues, country, or rock players, so they often use heavier gauge strings, which provide a meatier tone. Wound third strings are not uncommon in the jazz world, and while these strings are definitely bend-resistant, they help define the classic jazz guitar tone.

Get in Tune

16 First things first: Play track 16 and tune your guitar to mine. That way, you can play along with the audio and sound great.

Recording Credits

John Shank, engineer
Les Wise, guitar
Craig Fisher, piano

Luther Yuze, bass
Joe Brencatto, drums

Arpeggio Substitutions

Arpeggios are a great technique to have at your disposal when improvising and soloing. Yet simply knowing the right notes isn't really enough to create a good solo—you can't just string together a bunch of arpeggios, one for each chord, and expect the whole thing to sound solid; you need to know how to apply arpeggios, creatively and efficiently.

In this chapter, we'll focus on a solo technique known in jazz circles as *arpeggio substitutions.* My solo relies on it heavily. In the process of breaking down my solo, we'll learn a number of arpeggio and substitution devices used by such vaunted jazz guitarists as Wes Montgomery, Jimmy Raney, Johnny Smith, Kenny Burrell, and Jim Hall—and even a riff or two favored by sax great Charlie Parker.

Arpeggio Substitutions

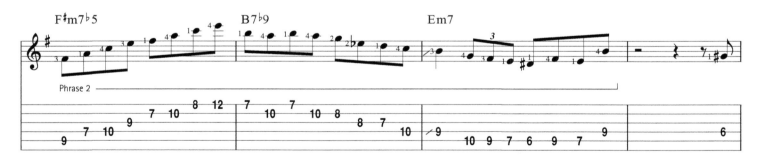

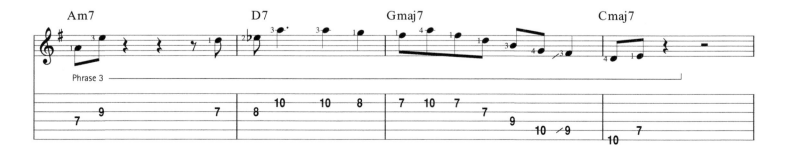

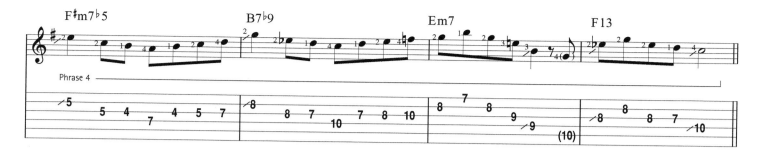

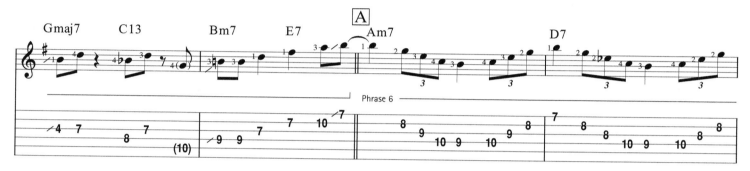

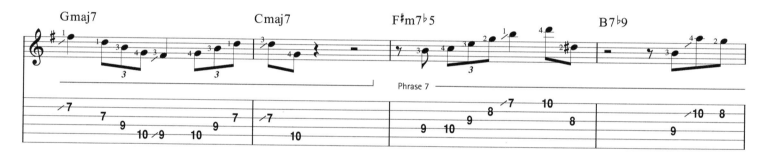

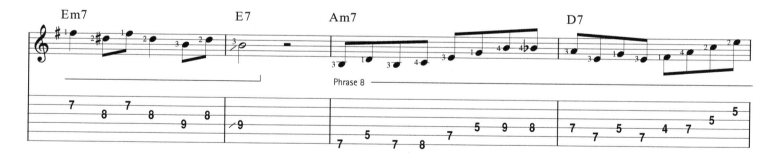

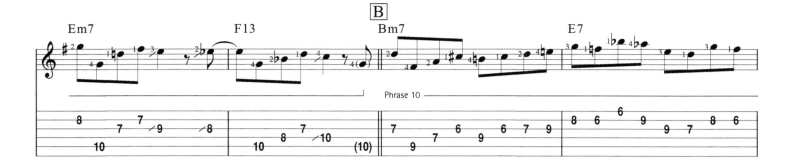

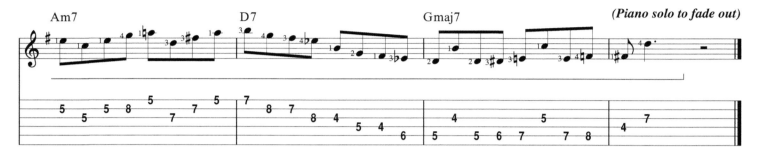

The Solo

Phrase 1

Our tune is in the key of G. If we look at the form, there's an A section that's sixteen bars long, followed by a B section that's six bars long. Then the whole form repeats; and that's our song.

Looking at Phrase 1, we see the chord progression Am7 to D7 to Gmaj7. In harmonic theory, this is known as a *ii–V–I (two-five-one)* progression. This is going to be a recurring element in this tune—and throughout this book—so we need to start recognizing it.

One way to handle a ii–V–I progression like this—and this is a favorite technique of Wes Montgomery, among other players—is with the use of *triads*. In this phrase of my solo, you'll find there are actually two triads, or arpeggios, that are being used to satisfy the sound of Am7-to-D7. These triads aren't the ii and the V, as you might think, and they aren't played one-arpeggio-per-chord; rather, both arpeggios are played over each chord. The triads used are the IV and the V—in this case, C and D.

Practice Point 1: If you were to play just C and D triads and started on the root of both, you'd sound like you were playing over two different chords. We don't want that to happen, so what we do is *invert* the second triad—that means we start on a note other than the root. So over the Am7 chord, I use a C triad. (Now, remember I'm referring to the triad, C–E–G, but we're also adding the octave, giving us four notes.) Then I play a D triad, inverted so that I begin on the 3rd (F♯) of the chord.

Practice Point 2: Now the rhythm moves into the D7 chord, but I'm treating this as part of a larger ii–V progression, so I continue to play the C and D triads. Actually, I lead into my C triad with an *approach note*, B, and then after the C triad, I play just a fragment of a D triad. My fragment again starts on the 3rd (F♯) of the D triad, then moves up to the 5th, using G as a passing note in between.

Practice Point 3: Now I hit the G chord and resolve the phrase with a few choice chord tones. This is followed by a Cmaj7 chord—the IV chord of the progression—but I just hold a note from the previous measure, so I don't really react to this chord at all.

So, any time we have a ii–V progression, we can use the IV and V chords of the key to solo over it. This is a very, very good device—a powerful tool. I highly recommend recording your own ii–V progressions (for example, Am7–D7 in the key of G) and practicing your IV and V chord inversions (e.g., C and D) across the fretboard.

Phrase 2

Phrase 2 begins on an F#m7♭5 chord, moves to B7♭9, and then to Em7. This is known as a *minor ii–V–i progression*; in effect, we're now moving—temporarily—into the key area of E minor. So how do we approach this slightly more intimidating ii–V–i? Once again, Wes Montgomery and the others provide us with some options.

Practice Point 1: There are several scale substitutes we can utilize for a minor ii–V–i progression. One of them would be to use a harmonic minor scale from the key area, E minor. However, we'll try something else here: One of Wes's favorite substitutes in this situation is based on the fact that the chord F#m7♭5 is a *plural* of another chord. That means it has the same notes—or almost the same notes—as another chord of another name. And in this particular case, F#m7♭5 has all the same notes as Am6. So, if we take an A minor arpeggio, and we add the 6th (F#), it works great over this chord.

Technically, the arpeggio I use in this phrase is as much an F#m7♭5 chord as it is an Am6 chord, but many guitarists find it easier to think of it as an Am6. The Am6 sound over an F#m7♭5 chord is a substitute Wes would use, and we can utilize it, too. A lot of times you can forget the 6th degree altogether and simply play an A minor lick for an F#m7♭5 chord—maybe even an A minor pentatonic. Wes would use substitutes such as this, and so would Jimmy Raney and Johnny Smith.

Practice Point 2: We have several things happening over the B7♭9. Primarily, we have the basic notes of the arpeggio: the root and flatted 7th of B. But over the second half of the measure, we also have a group of notes that aren't in a B7 chord. What we're using here is the *flat-five substitute* for B7.

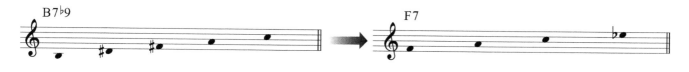

For any dominant seventh chord like B7♭9, we can substitute the dominant seventh chord built from its flatted 5th. In this case, the ♭5 of B would be an F natural. So we can play an F7, and it will give us the altered B7 chord sound we're looking for. Actually, I play an F9 arpeggio fragment here: G, E♭, D, then C.

Practice Point 3: Here I resolve inward to an E minor. What I primarily use is a fragment of the E natural minor scale, and then I use the major 7th (D#) and the 9th (F#) as *target notes* before I play the root and the 5th.

Phrase 3

With Phrase 3, we return to our original progression, Am7–D7–Gmaj7–Cmaj7. This time, we'll use fewer notes to create a question-and-answer, or *call-and-response,* effect—another typical jazz device. In call-and-response phrasing, a guitarist will play a little fragment or idea and then play it again at a higher or lower pitch level to satisfy the sound of the next chord or key. This creates interest for listeners because there's a melody that they can grasp.

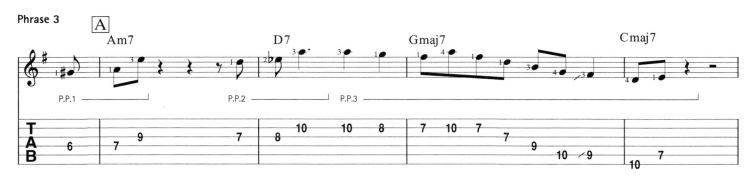

Practice Point 1: This is the musical "call," or question, over the Am7 chord.

Practice Point 2: This is the "response," or answer, over the D7 chord.

Practice Point 3: Now, anticipating the Gmaj7 chord of the next measure, I play A again, and resolve to G. Then, over the Gmaj7 chord, I play a full major ninth arpeggio.

Simple arpeggios like this—major sevenths, minor sevenths, and dominant sevenths—are another device that Wes Montgomery, Jimmy Raney, and Johnny Smith used often. They're a very, very important tool to utilize when improvising. Don't forget to learn them. You should learn to play your seventh chord arpeggios over a barre chord first. Then you should be able to add the 9th scale degree to complete the ninth arpeggio.

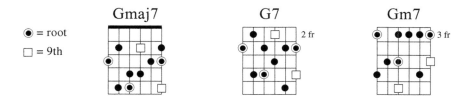

Phrase 4

Next we have our familiar minor ii–V–i progression, F#m7b5–B7b9–Em7. This time we'll try another tool to use over this progression: *moving up in minor thirds.* Let's see how it works.

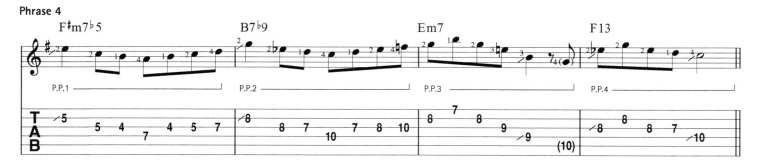

Practice Point 1: We learned earlier that a good substitute for F#m7b5 is an Am6 chord. Well, here's another one: D9. Except for its root, a D9 chord has the same notes as Am6 and F#m7b5.

So we can use any D9 shape to give us this sound. And that's what I do here: I play a combination arpeggio and scale fragment.

Practice Point 2: For our B7 chord, we'll make another ♭5 substitution, replacing it with F9. But something else is going to happen here: you'll notice that the distance from D9 to F9 is a minor third interval. So I can take the phrase I just played in Practice Point 1, based on D9, and move it up a minor third—four frets. This gives us a really neat sound that all jazz players utilize. Plus, we've stated a question and answer.

Practice Point 3: We'll continue our question-and-answer phrasing for Em and F13, but in this case using another melodic idea. Over the Em7 chord, I play a fragment of an Em arpeggio.

Practice Point 4: Now I want to keep this little melody going, so when we get to the F13, I simply continue the phrasing.

Remember, when you see an F13 chord, it's really just an F7 chord with a couple of extra tones. Theoretically, a thirteenth chord consists of the root, 3rd, 5th, ♭7th, 9th, 11th, and 13th—but that's seven notes, and we only have six notes on the guitar. And we really don't need all of them anyway. In the case of a thirteenth chord, we have the 13th added, and sometimes the 9th is included, too.

Phrase 5

Now we arrive at our B section, which uses a new chord progression that basically descends through a cycle of fifths (you'll find a few ii–V's in here, too). Phrase 5 is typical of something Jimmy Raney might play. It's a *vertical style* of playing, where I play right up an arpeggio, then right back down—or I climb up the arpeggio, take a step back, then continue to climb.

Phrase 5

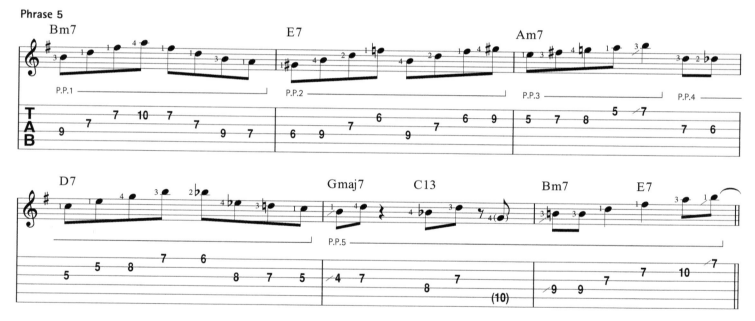

Practice Point 1: To start, I play up and down a Bm7 arpeggio.

Practice Point 2: Then I come to my E7 arpeggio, to which I'm adding a flatted 9th. I climb up, take a step back, then climb again. These are actually A harmonic minor scale fragments—E is the V chord of A minor—but they're played vertically, using arpeggios based on the harmonized version of this scale. Again, this is very typical of Jimmy Raney.

Practice Point 3: Here we have an Am7 chord, which is headed to D7 and G major again. And so we have a scale source that we're dealing with; a ii–V–I progression in the key of G. So I use a G major scale fragment over this chord.

Practice Point 4: Now I do a quick chromatic move—D to D♭—followed by an arpeggio that hits all the extensions of a D13 chord: 7th (C), 9th (E), 11th (G), and 13th (B).

This is another common sound that Wes Montgomery would use, and it's very typical of Jimmy Raney and George Benson, too. We've used scale tones and arpeggios—but in this case, all extensions: 7, 9, 11, and 13. How did we accomplish this? We used an interesting technique. It just so happens that to create all the extensions—the flatted 7th (C), the 9th (E), the 11th (G), and the 13th (B)—we just need to play a major seventh arpeggio a whole step down. So we can play a Cmaj7 arpeggio in place of a D7 arpeggio, and we'll get all the extensions of a D13 chord.

Then I lower some of these extensions as I head downward, playing the ♯5th (B♭), ♭9th (E♭), root (D), and ♭7th (C).

Practice Point 5: Over the quick chord change that wraps up this phrase, Gmaj7–C13–Bm7–E7, I play some recurring figures that work over each chord. Over Gmaj7, I play B and D. Over C13, I play B♭ and D. Then over Bm7 to E7, I play B, D, F♯, and A—a Bm7 arpeggio.

Phrase 6

Most beginning improvisers don't use the quarter note that much; they prefer high-speed, fancy licks. But when improvising, you'll notice that Wes, Jimmy Raney, and other players favor the use of the quarter note on occasion. They might be soloing along, and then suddenly they'll just play four quarter notes in a row. So quarter notes can be an effective tool.

In Phrase 6, we have our major ii–V–I progression again, Am7–D7–Gmaj7. Instead of just playing more eighth-note lines, I combine quarter notes with triplets for a real change of pace. Plus, I try some new chord substitution ideas involving major seventh arpeggios.

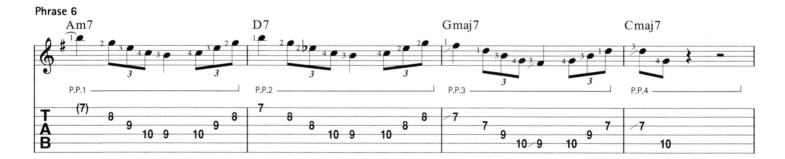

Practice Point 1: One device Wes Montgomery would often utilize when playing in quarter notes is the major seventh arpeggio. Wes was particularly fond of substituting a *major seventh* arpeggio in place of its *relative minor*. And that's just what I do here: I have an Am7 chord, but on top of it I play a Cmaj7 arpeggio, which fits quite well. Basically, it creates an Am9 sound.

Practice Point 2: For the D7 chord, I use something a little different. I play a Cmaj7 arpeggio, except I flat the 3rd, making it a C minor triad with a major 7th—i.e., Cm(maj7). That works well over a D13 with a ♭9, a substitution or extension for the D7 chord.

Also, I make use of the call-and-response technique here again.

Practice Point 3: When I get to the Gmaj7, I play the same idea again, this time using a Gmaj7 arpeggio. This is effective because repetition attracts the listener's attention. Wes used this technique all the time.

Practice Point 4: Over the Cmaj7 chord, I resolve to an E, then G.

So to summarize, for Am7, we're using a Cmaj7 arpeggio. For D7 (or D13♭9), we're using a Cm(maj7) arpeggio—which I think of as a Cmaj7 arpeggio with a ♭3. And then for Gmaj7, we're just using our Gmaj7 arpeggio. If you want to sound like Johnny Smith, Jimmy Raney, or Wes Montgomery, use those major seventh arpeggios over minor chords—and over the major chords, too. It's a very nice, open sound.

Phrase 7

In Phrase 7, we have our minor ii–V–i progression again, F♯m7♭5–B7♭9–Em7. I'm going to borrow some harmonic concepts from earlier phrases to expand on the chord substitutions we've already learned—and add in a little something new.

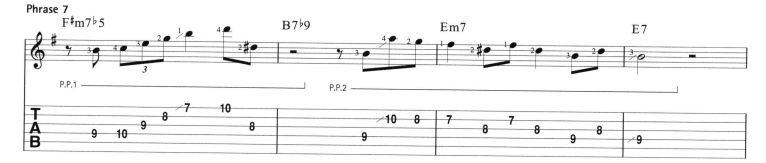

Practice Point 1: We learned earlier that F♯m7♭5 is a synonym of Am6, and that D9 is likewise an appropriate substitute. But you'll notice that we've now started using Cmaj7 and Cm(maj7) to give us the sound of Am7 to D7. So why not continue to use this sound?

Over the F♯m7♭5 chord, I play a Cmaj7 arpeggio (with a 9th added). Then I flat the 3rd, making it Cm(maj7), and this note (E♭) happens to be the harmonic equivalent of the major 3rd (D♯) of B7♭9.

Practice Point 2: From there, we move on to the Em7 chord. There are several substitutes for a minor seventh chord. One that jazz players like to use—it adds kind of a mystic sound—is the 9th and the *major* 7th over the chord. Wes Montgomery liked this sound, and it's what I use here.

Another way to look at this sound is as a Gmaj7 arpeggio with a sharp 5th; this would be a plural to Em(maj9). So, if you're looking for that mystic sound over a minor seventh chord like Em7, just play a maj7♯5 arpeggio a minor third (four frets) higher—in this case, Gmaj7♯5.

I should mention that there are three very important tones to play over a minor chord in jazz. One of those is the 9th of the minor chord; another is the major 7th; the last is the 6th. These are called *color tones.* They're real attention-getting tones; try finding shapes that incorporate these tones, and then start adding them in to your solos.

Phrase 8

In Phrase 8, I use basic scale forms and chromatics to tackle our familiar major ii–V–I progression in G. This phrase was influenced by Charlie Parker, especially the concept of *targeting chromaticism*, where chord tones are arrived at chromatically.

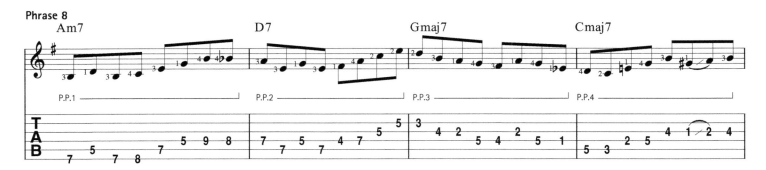

Practice Point 1: Over the Am7 chord, I start with a scale fragment from a basic G major scale. Then, I do something unusual: I add a B♭. This B♭ is the chromatic transition note—something you'll see throughout this solo and the other solos in this book. A *transition note* is a note used to approach a strong chord tone, or target note, usually by a half step. In this case, the B♭ is used to approach the 5th (A) of the next chord, which is D7.

Practice Point 2: Over the D7 chord, I start with another scale figure, and then I climb up a D9 arpeggio—a vertical sound.

Practice Point 3: Then I move down a Gmaj9 arpeggio. Notice that with the last note of this pattern, I'm setting up the C major pattern in the next measure with another transition note. I half-step approach the first note of the next measure, the 9th (D) of a Cmaj9 arpeggio, with the note E♭.

Practice Point 4: With the Cmaj7 chord, you see the interjection of a G♯, which is the ♯5th of the chord. This note is used to set up the A—the 6th of the chord, a strong melodic tone.

The *sharp five* is another simple, common substitute. When playing over a Cmaj7 chord—or any major chord—we can always utilize the raised or lowered 5th in place of the 4th degree of a major scale. These are more color tones you should be aware of.

Phrase 9

In Phrase 9, I continue some of the melodic phrasing I began over the Cmaj7 chord.

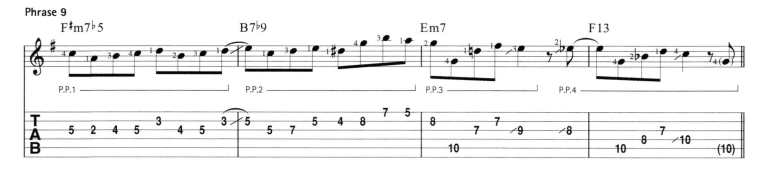

Practice Point 1: Again, for F♯m7♭5, I substitute the Am or D9 arpeggios.

Practice Point 2: Over B7♭9, I continue the idea, reaching the 3rd (D♯) of the chord.

Practice Point 3: Basically, an Em7 arpeggio.

Practice Point 4: Here, the chord goes to F13, but I want to keep this melody going, so I use the call-and-response technique.

Phrase 10

Phrase 10 wraps up the solo over the song's B section, the descending circle-of-fifths chord pattern. One of the interesting melodic techniques here is when I use a ♭9th to create a diminished sound.

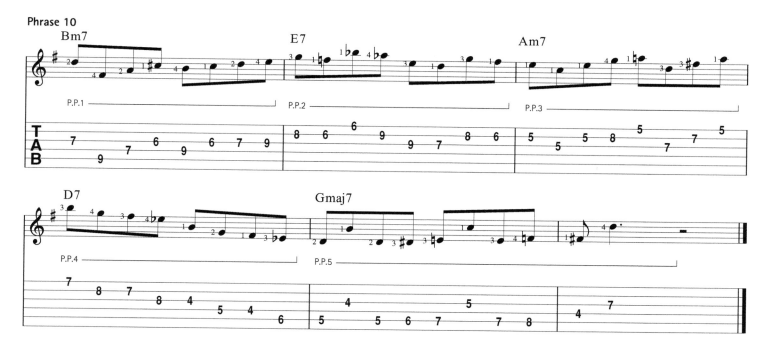

Practice Point 1: Over the Bm7 chord, I play a Bm9 arpeggio modeled after the previous phrase, then a lick right out of a B minor scale.

Practice Point 2: Over E7, I add the ♭9 (F) and ♭5 (B♭), which give me that diminished sound.

Practice Point 3: Over Am7, I use our two triads again: C and D.

Practice Point 4: Over D7, I play a short D13♭9 sort of lick, repeated at the octave.

Practice Point 5: I wrap up the solo over Gmaj7 with some string-skipping. Notice the little melody on the third string—B, C, D. This really pulls the line together.

Everything We've Learned So Far

We've covered a lot of ideas in this chapter. Here are some highlights:

- We can use triads to satisfy the sound of seventh chords.

- We don't have to use the specific arpeggio like Am7 for Am7, and D7 for D7, but we can utilize combinations of triads like C and D for Am7-to-D7.

- We can substitute Am6 or D9 for F#m7♭5.

- We can substitute another arpeggio or melodic shape a ♭5th above any dominant seventh chord.

- We can use color tones, such as the 9th, the major 7th, and the 6th.

- We can use call and response, where we play a fragment or idea and then repeat it at the octave or in another key to satisfy the next chord.

- We can use major seventh arpeggios, which have a very pleasant sound, in a variety of situations.

- We can vary our rhythms—occasionally using quarter notes for emphasis, as opposed to always using eighth notes.

Now go ahead and use all these techniques over the rhythm section on track 2, and have fun!

2 Scale Substitutions

In this chapter, I'll explain scale substitutions and something I refer to as *horizontal lines:* solo or melody lines that are scalar in nature. (When I refer to vertical lines, I mean arpeggios.)

This solo is in the style of guitarists like Tal Farlow, Jim Hall, Joe Pass, and Herb Ellis. Of course, these players all use a combination of scales *and* arpeggios when they improvise, but in this discussion I'll emphasize some of the scales and scale fragments—the horizontal lines—that they're known for.

Scale Substitutions

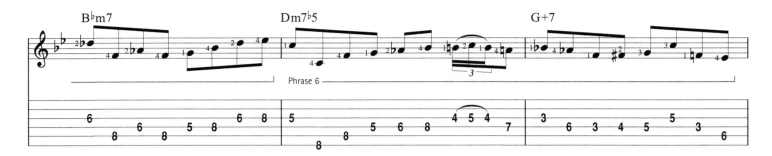

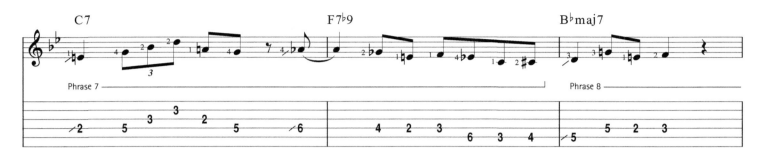

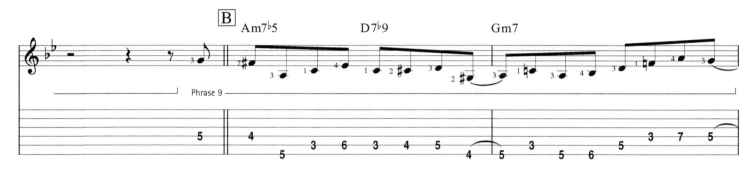

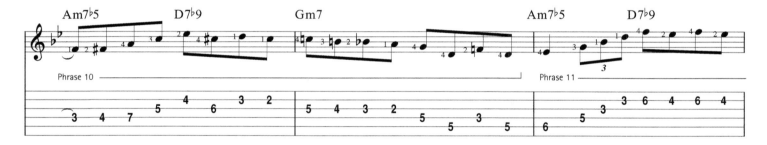

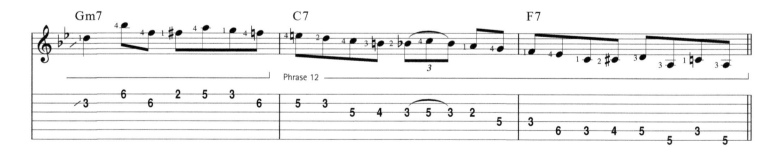

The Solo

Phrase 1

Our tune is in the key of B♭ major, and the form is AABA, with each section being eight bars long. In the previous chapter, we dealt with ii–V–I progressions quite a lot, and we'll find them in this tune, too. But this song starts off with something different: a *major-to-minor* chord change—specifically, B♭maj7 to B♭m7. There are several ways to accomplish this type of change. I'll show you what I played here, and then I'll explain a few alternatives.

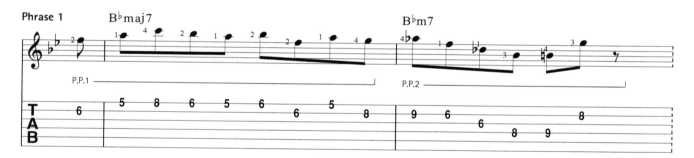

Practice Point 1: Over the B♭maj7 chord, I play a B♭ major scale fragment.

Practice Point 2: Over the B♭m7 chord, I play a B♭m7 arpeggio. I add one note outside the B♭ minor scale—B♮— and move upwards to G, the 6th degree. This gives us a B♭m13♭9 sound.

Anytime you come across a major-to-minor chord change like this, you've got several options, besides what I just played. One option is to play a major scale pattern of some kind for the major chord, and then simply flat the 3rd of that idea for the minor chord, leaving everything else in place. By flatting the 3rd of a B♭ major scale, we now are playing a B♭ melodic minor scale.

Another option we have is to take our major pattern and move it up a minor third. For example, if I play Bb major and then move it up a minor third, I'm now playing another scale: Db major. By playing a Db major scale (or Dbmaj7 arpeggio) over Bb minor, what I'm really doing is bringing out the sound of Bbm9.

Anytime you want a minor sound, you can simply play a major scale a minor third higher. This is a very common sound used by a lot of jazz players. Jim Hall and Joe Pass—Joe, especially—like that sound. It's a very strong sound when improvising.

Phrase 2

The next progression we come upon is Dm7b5–G7. Anytime we have a dominant seventh chord of some kind, like G7, and I play a G+7, a G7b5, or a G7#9 or b9—or any combination of those—that's called *altered tension.* And we use several scales to satisfy that sound. In this case, the altered chord is part of a minor ii–V progression, so I'm going to choose a scale based on that fact.

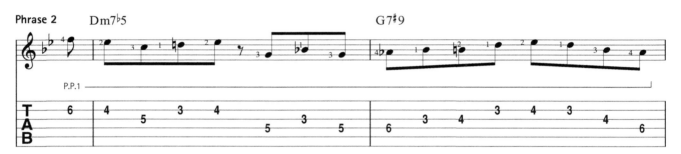

Practice Point 1: One important scale we can utilize for any minor ii–V progression like this is the harmonic minor scale based on the implied tonic, or i chord—in this case, C harmonic minor. That's what I do here.

Phrase 3

In this phrase, we have a C7 chord—a dominant seventh—for two measures. We can use several things to satisfy this sound.

Practice Point 1: First of all, the C7 or C9 chords have a plural: Gm7 or Gm6. So, while the band is playing a C7 or a C9 chord, not only can we play C7 or C9 arpeggios, but we can also play Gm7 or Gm6 ideas—or we would utilize a scale based on this plurality. Specifically, we can use a melodic minor scale a fifth higher than any dominant seventh chord that we play.

Think about it this way: if C is the V chord, then the ii chord would be Gm, so this is the melodic minor scale based on the ii chord. So, a fifth higher than C is G. When the band plays C7, we can play the G melodic minor scale. (Also remember, a melodic minor scale is nothing more than a major scale with a flatted 3rd; to get a G melodic minor scale, just take a G major scale and flat the 3rd.)

That scale is very commonly used in improvising. Jazz players such as Herb Ellis, Jim Hall, Tal Farlow, and Joe Pass use this substitution principle all the time.

Phrase 4

In Phrase 4, we see an F7 chord, plus a quick ii–V progression that substitutes for the F7: a Cm7–F7 change. I basically treat this as one long F7 chord played for two bars. There are several scale substitutes we can utilize over a dominant chord like this, and the one I opted for is the one we just learned: the melodic minor scale a fifth higher.

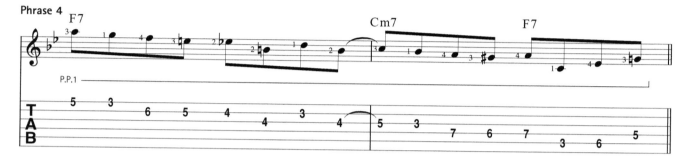

Practice Point 1: A fifth higher than F7 is C minor, so we can use a C melodic minor scale here, and this will give us the sound of our F7 or F9 chord.

Use of the melodic minor scale over dominant chords is a very powerful tool. A lot of times, it will even occur in blues tunes—e.g., when we see an F7 or an F13 chord, we play C melodic minor.

You'll notice in these licks that we also make use of *passing tones* or *chromatic notes* connecting some of our chord tones. B♭, for instance, would be the fourth degree of an F chord; it's used to connect the 5th (C) with the 3rd (A). G♯ is used as a chromatic lower neighbor to the 3rd (A) of the F chord.

Phrase 5

In Phrase 5, we return to our song's A section and the major-to-minor chord change. Another great substitute we can utilize for the minor chord (B♭m7) in this progression is the dominant seventh arpeggio—actually, seventh or ninth—a fourth higher. Let's see how that works.

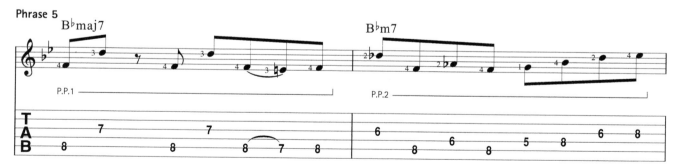

Practice Point 1: Over the B♭maj7 chord, I'm using primarily a B♭ major scale.

Practice Point 2: Over the B♭m7 chord, I'm going to use the dominant seventh chord a fourth higher. So, what's a fourth higher than B♭m7? It's E♭7. So we play an E♭7 arpeggio or scale fragment—which is the equivalent of a B♭ melodic minor scale.

Phrase 6

In Phrase 6, we come across another Dm7♭5 to altered G7 progression—in other words, a minor ii–V chord change. Earlier in the tune when we encountered this progression, we used the harmonic minor scale based on the minor i chord that the progression was heading to—C harmonic minor. In this case, we're going to try something different: we'll use a melodic minor scale a minor third higher than the ii chord (Dm7♭5).

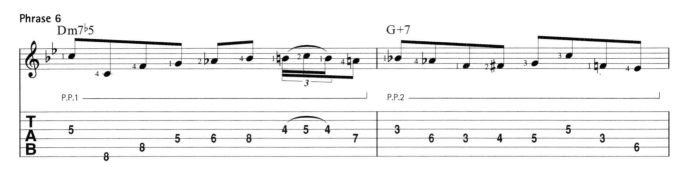

Practice Point 1: A minor third higher than D is F, so we're going to play an F melodic minor scale fragment here. The F melodic minor scale (or Fm6 chord) has the same notes as Dm7♭5, so when the band plays Dm7♭5, I can play an F melodic minor scale, and that sound will work perfectly.

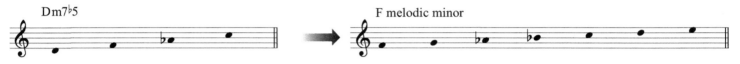

Commercial or fusion guitar players who use pentatonic scales can also play out of F minor pentatonic when the band plays Dm7♭5.

Practice Point 2: Over the G7 chord, I'm going to continue to use F melodic minor, giving us the sound of G7 altered. This, by the way, is a very common sound in jazz. It's called the *subdominant minor*. Because the G7 resolves to C7 in the next phrase, it's acting as the V chord of C. In the key of C, the subdominant (IV) chord is F, and if we make that chord minor, it becomes subdominant minor. This subdominant minor actually works like a substitute for the dominant chord in certain progressions, pulling you back to the tonic, like this:

So, when you're playing in any key and make the IV chord minor, it will act as a V chord, even though you're on the IV chord. And you can use this scale as a substitute anytime you're playing over a dominant seventh chord.

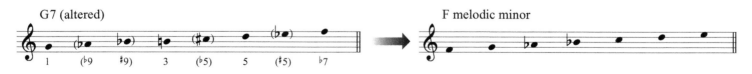

Now, another way to get the F minor sound is to play an A♭ major scale or arpeggio instead—because the A♭maj7 includes the same notes as Fm9. This means that when you come to a dominant seventh chord like G7, you also have the option of playing the major scale or arpeggio a half step higher.

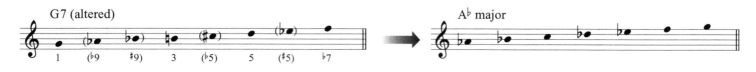

22

So when you see a G7 chord, you can play F minor licks (melodic or pentatonic) or A♭ major ideas. Joe Pass, Jim Hall, and Tal Farlow did this all the time. These are things you can utilize to create that flow, that power, that continuity in your solo.

Phrase 7

In this phrase, our chord progression is C7 to F7♭9.

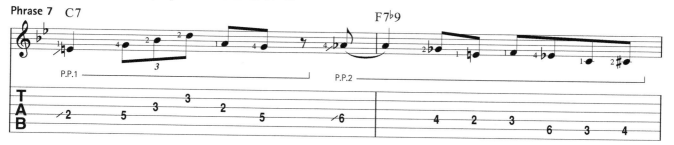

Practice Point 1: For the C7 chord, I have three or four basic choices. C7 is the V chord in the key of F, so I could play an F major scale. In this case, though, what I use is the melodic minor scale a fifth higher—a Gm7 arpeggio or a G minor scale fragment. This G minor scale gives us that C9 or C13 kind of sound.

Practice Point 2: The next chord is F7♭9. Any time F7 acts as the V chord—which in this case it does because we're going to B♭maj7—we can add altered notes, meaning a raised or lowered 5th or 9th. To get these altered tones, I play the major scale a half step higher—the F♯ major scale—just as I suggested in the previous phrase (e.g., playing an A♭ major scale over a G+7 chord).

Phrase 8

This phrase wraps up our A section on a B♭maj7 chord. I kept this one pretty simple.

Practice Point 1: Over the B♭maj7 chord, I play the 3rd (D) and 5th (F), using G and E as surrounding tones.

Phrase 9

Now we're moving into the B section, or bridge, of the tune. In the bridge, our progression is Am7♭5–D7♭9–Gm7: a minor ii–V–i progression in which the ii and the V chords occupy only two beats each.

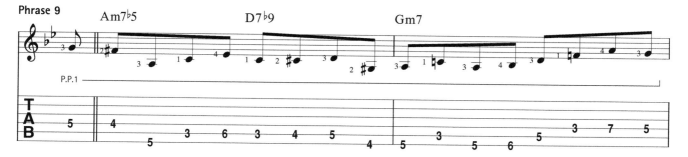

Practice Point 1: In this particular instance, we can use several scales. For Am7♭5, we can use a melodic minor scale a minor third higher—C melodic minor. And then over the D7♭9 chord, we can just continue playing our C melodic minor scale; this is probably a good idea since we only have one measure to play over both chords. We could also use a harmonic minor scale based on the i chord of the progression—G harmonic minor.

These scales are very characteristic of Jim Hall, Joe Pass, Herb Ellis, or Tal Farlow's playing. These are scale subs that they utilize all the time when they see this chord progression, especially that melodic minor scale a minor third higher than the m7♭5 chord.

Phrase 10

Next, we repeat the same progression: Am7♭5–D7♭9–Gm7. In this phrase, I expand upon the substitution explained in Phrase 9.

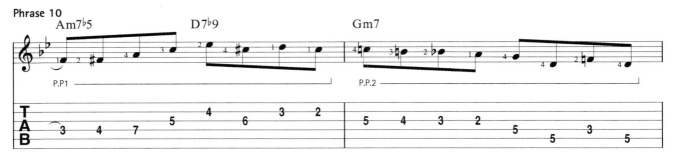

Practice Point 1: Over the Am7♭5 and D7♭9 chords, I play more C melodic minor ideas.

Practice Point 2: Over the Gm7 chord, I play a chromatic run followed by a pivot of the root (G) and ♭7th (F) around the 5th (D).

Phrase 11

In this phrase, we repeat the same progression again, and I throw in a new substitute: I play a minor third above the minor third of Am7♭5. In other words, I play an E♭maj7 or E♭maj9 arpeggio, or an E♭ major scale, instead of the C melodic minor.

Practice Point 1: Over the Am7♭5 and D7♭9 chords, I play an E♭maj9 idea.

Practice Point 2: Over the Gm7 chord, I go back to the G melodic minor scale.

Phrase 12

For the C7 and F7 chords at the end of this bridge, the simplest thing to play is the scale source.

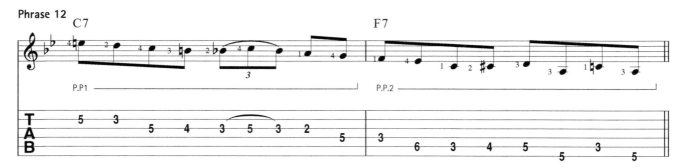

Practice Point 1: Because C7 is the V of the key of F, I play an F major scale here, adding a chromatic note, B, to get to the B♭.

Practice Point 2: Over the F7 chord, I go back to emphasizing the C melodic minor scale. (This F7 acts as a V chord to the B♭maj7 that follows.)

Phrase 13

Now we're back to our last A section, with the major-to-minor chord change.

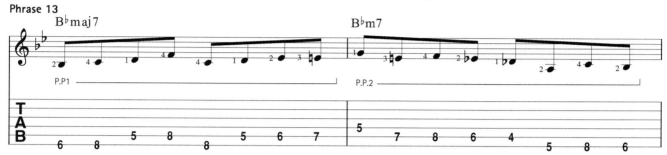

Practice Point 1: As jazz players, we can do several things over a major seventh chord like B♭maj7. The major scale itself has seven notes, plus the octave, which gives us eight notes total—this works our great if we're playing an eighth-note line. But keep in mind, most jazz players don't play the fourth degree in the major scale. To make up for this missing note, they'll add a color tone: a ♭5 or a ♯5.

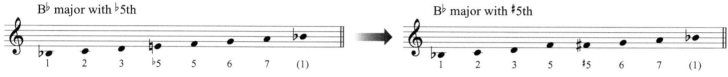

Again, color tones give a line strength and character. (Note: Even though we're playing a sharped or flatted 5th, the band can still be playing a regular maj7 chord.) Jazz players will often use these particular notes to target the 5th, playing the flat or raised 5th first, then the natural 5th. This is an extremely important device used by Joe Pass, Herb Ellis, Tal Farlow—all of them. They make use of this sort of targeting technique, raising or lowering the 5th and then returning to the natural 5th.

In this phrase, you'll notice that I play the 4th, then the ♭5th, for a chromatic effect.

Practice Point 2: Next, over the B♭m7 chord, I use a B♭ melodic minor scale. Notice the A♮. In a B♭m7 chord, the 7th (A♭) is minor, but in the melodic minor scale, we use the major 7th (A). Remember: a B♭ melodic minor scale is a major scale with a flatted 3rd.

The last few notes set up a little question and answer, which we'll satisfy over next chord, Dm7♭5.

Phrase 14

With this phrase, we'll answer the melodic question just posed.

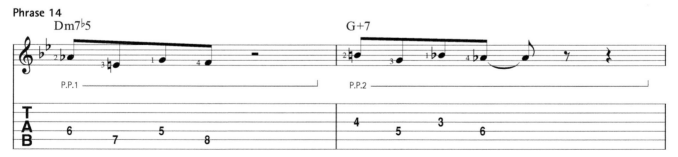

Practice Point 1: Over the Dm7♭5, we want to bring out the sound of that chord. One way to do that is to look for some kind of plurality—in this case, an Fm6 chord. So we can use an F melodic minor scale to satisfy the sound of that chord.

Practice Point 2: Over the G+7 chord, we continue the question-and-answer idea.

As I mentioned previously, the question-and-answer technique is very important and something that Joe Pass, Jim Hall, Herb Ellis, Tal Farlow—all of them—make use of to create interest for the listener.

Phrase 15

In this phrase, I play over Cm7 going to F7—a ii-V progression in B♭. Now I'm going to try out a new substitute for a V7 chord using the melodic minor scale.

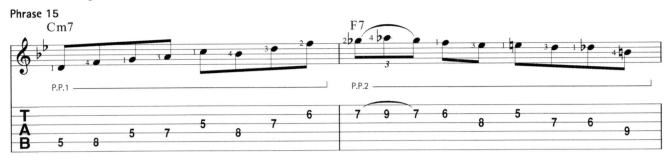

Practice Point 1: Because these two chords, Cm7 and F7, are leading to a B♭maj7 chord in the next phrase, we can use a B♭ major scale and it will work perfectly here. So that's what I do over this Cm7 chord.

Practice Point 2: Another substitute used a great deal by Joe Pass and Wes Montgomery in situations like this is a melodic minor scale a half step above the dominant seventh chord. I've talked before about using the *major scale* a half step higher than a dominant chord; now we're talking about substituting a *melodic minor* scale in the same situation. Over the F7 chord, we'll use an F♯ melodic minor scale—this will give us an F7 with a ♭9/♯9 sound.

Keep in mind that the melodic minor scale is just a major scale with a flatted 3rd. So when substituting for the dominant seventh chord like this, whether we use the major scale a half step higher, or the melodic minor scale, the difference is only one note: the 3rd.

Phrase 16

In these last two measures, we have B♭maj7-G7-Cm7-F7. This particular sequence is called a *turnaround*. A turnaround is a progression that appears at the end of a song or song section that's used to get back to the beginning. Typically, it leads us strongly back to, and sets us up for, the first chord of the tune. In this case, the first chord of the tune is B♭. So in our turnaround, we play B♭, the I chord, then G7, the VI chord, then Cm, the ii chord; followed by F7, the V chord. And the F7 resolves back to B♭ when the tune repeats. This is a very common I-VI-ii-V-I turnaround.

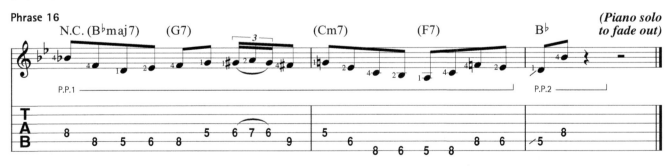

Practice Point 1: We could do several things here. For one, we could just play a B♭ major scale for the entire progression. That's one possibility that a lot of jazz players would utilize. Secondly, we could add some kind of scale source that would draw out the sound of our G7. Notice that G7 is the V of Cm; it has a V-to-i relationship to Cm, even though we're really in the key of B♭. So we could substitute some scale that would create altered tension over the G7. And notice as we go on, we come to F7. Again, F7 is the V of B♭, so we could use altered tension there as well. And we've learned that we can use several things for altered tension—in particular, a major scale or a melodic minor scale a half a step higher.

However, there's another device that a lot of jazz players like to use over a turnaround like this. Notice that the B♭maj7, Cm7, and F7 all belong to a B♭ major scale, but G7 doesn't belong to that particular scale. And notice that the 3rd of the G7 chord is a B♮, but there's no B♮ in a B♭ major scale.

So, what many jazz players will do is play a B♭ major scale for the first two beats, and then they will raise their hand a half a step to a B major scale. And this B major scale will emphasize the B, which is the 3rd of G7.

Now, the one thing you'll notice is that when I play a B major scale for G7, I do get the B♮ but I also get an F♯. And an F♯ is a major 7th over a dominant seventh chord. Don't worry about that. A lot of saxophone players use this particular tone in passing. Since the chord is only occurring for two beats, it won't affect our improvising. This is a very common technique.

Practice Point 2: I wrap the solo up on a B♭ chord. This is the beginning of the tune again, and the piano takes over from here.

That's All There Is

In this chapter, we've learned quite a few useful tools. We understand various ways to handle a major-to-minor chord change. We also know about using a major scale or a melodic minor scale a half step higher than our target chord. And we know about using a melodic minor scale a fifth higher or a minor third higher than our target chord—depending on the kind of chord we're playing.

We've covered quite a lot of ground. Play over the backup track below, then take some standards and jazz tunes and work with them using these techniques. Good luck, and enjoy.

3 Tension and Resolution

In this chapter, I'll cover some very important techniques revolving around the musical concepts of *tension* and *resolution*. I'll also show you more ways to solo over the very common ii–V–I chord progression. Plus, I'll take a look at some of the melodic devices used by artists such as Pat Martino, George Benson, and Wes Montgomery.

Natural and Altered Tension

I'll begin with the use of tension and resolution. In a ii–V–I progression, there is one point where tension is used a great deal. This is where the V chord—usually played as a dominant seventh—resolves to the I chord. This dominant seventh (V7) chord is extremely important to us as improvisers.

There are two types of dominant seventh chords: chords with natural tension, such as a seventh, ninth, or thirteenth chord; and chords with altered tension, such as a seventh chord with a raised or flatted 5th or 9th. This is important because these different types of dominant seventh chords act different ways in chord progressions.

Functioning vs. Nonfunctioning Dominant Chords

One of the very important concepts that Pat Martino, George Benson, and Wes Montgomery use when they're improvising is that when they encounter a dominant seventh chord that is the V of the next chord, such as in a ii–V–I, they choose a scale that will create altered tension over the V chord. This altered tension will create interest for the listener and, more importantly, guide the listener through the solo. And it's critical that we be able to lead the listener through the solo.

Anytime we encounter a dominant seventh chord of any kind, if it is the V of the next chord, we consider it a *functioning* dominant seventh chord. If it is not the V of the next chord, we consider it nonfunctioning. If it is a functioning dominant seventh, we can play a scale that gives us either natural or altered tension. If it is a nonfunctioning dominant seventh, then we'll want to play a scale that will give us a natural tension over the chord.

Some songs don't have ii–V–I progressions; they may only have a dominant seventh chord that's moving into a new tonal area. But any time we find a dominant seventh chord that is the V of the next chord, it is an ideal situation in which to use altered tension.

Creating Altered Tension

Now, how do we create altered tension over this dominant seventh chord? As we learned previously , when we encounter a dominant seventh chord, we can play:

- a melodic minor scale a half-step higher than the root of the chord
- a major scale a half step higher than the root of the chord

So, if we're in the key of C and have a G7 chord and want to play G7 altered (G7$\flat$5, G+7, G7$\flat$9, G7$\sharp$9, etc.), we can play G$\sharp$ or A$\flat$ melodic minor. Or we can play G$\sharp$ or A$\flat$ major.

But there are other scales we can utilize as well. We could also choose:

- the harmonic minor scale based on the i chord (a fourth above the root of V7)
- the harmonic minor scale based on the vi chord (a whole step above the root of V7)
- the melodic minor scale based on the ii chord (a fifth above the root of V7)
- the melodic minor scale based on the iv chord (a whole step below the root of V7)

So again, if we have a G7 and want an altered sound, we could play C harmonic minor, A harmonic minor, D melodic minor, or F melodic minor. These are just some of the scales we can utilize to create this tension.

What we're really concerned with is leading the listener through the solo, and these rules of altered tension work to accomplish this throughout the chord progression. If the progression goes Cmaj7–A7–Dm7–G7, the A7 acts as the V of Dm7, so there's a V-to-I relationship. Then there is another V-to-I relationship when G7 returns to Cmaj7. So methods of creating altered tension can be used over each of these V-to-I resolutions within the chord progression. Because I can use altered tension over each of these chords, the listener can hear the chord progression in the solo, even without chords—if I were to play the solo lines by myself.

Altered Tension in Blues

Another place we can use this altered tension concept is in a blues tune. Let's say we're playing blues in the key of B♭—and remember, often, in blues, the chords are all dominant anyway. But still, the B♭ chord that we're on as we're soloing over the blues for the first four measures has a V-to-I relationship to E♭, which is the IV chord in the key of B♭. So I can play over the B♭ with a normal blues pattern for three measures, and then when I get to that fourth measure, switch scales to play something with altered tension. This allows me to lead the listener to the IV chord.

And here's another way to use altered tension in a blues tune: In a minor blues, we play four measures of the minor i chord. But to use altered tension, in the fourth measure of the minor i chord, we can change the chord to dominant. Even though the band is still playing that minor chord, the soloist can change it to a dominant seventh, and then play an altered tension scale over it.

Creating Natural Tension

Sometimes dominant seventh chords are nonfunctioning—they don't resolve in a typical V-to-I fashion—so we won't want to use altered tension in our solo lines. We'll want to use natural tension instead. (Actually, even if the dominant chord is functioning, we have the option of using natural tension.)

Now how do we play scales with natural tension over a dominant seventh chord? One thing we can do is choose a scale that won't give us all the alterations, or maybe a scale that will only give us the extensions that we need, primarily natural: the 9, 11, and 13.

One natural tension scale that is commonly used over a dominant seventh chord is a melodic minor scale a fifth higher than the root of the dominant seventh chord. I'll give examples of other natural tension options as we continue, but let's get to the solo.

Tension and Resolution

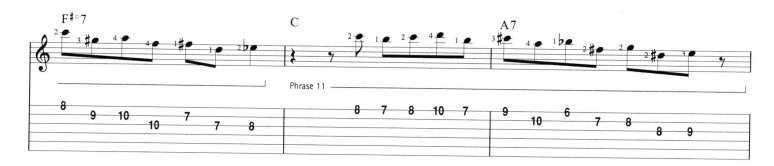

The Solo

Phrase 1

The song in this chapter is in the key of C and follows the form ABAC, with each section being eight bars long. We begin our first A section on two measures of a C major chord.

Practice Point 1: Even though this C chord is not a dominant of the chord that follows, I've used arpeggios alternating with chromatic lines to create a sense of tension.

Phrase 2

In Phrase 2, the chord progression moves to E7, a dominant seventh. To find out whether the E7 is "functioning" or not, we look ahead. While the chord immediately following—in the next phrase—is an Em7♭5, the chord after that is an A7. Since E7 is the V of A7, this is a functioning dominant seventh. (Think of Em7♭5 in the next phrase as a substitution; instead of two measures of A7, the progression Em7♭5–A7 is used. In fact, this will be a ii–V leading into the Dm7 chord that follows!)

Practice Point 1: Because this E7 chord lasts two measures, we can wait to set up or start leading ourselves into Em7♭5-to-A7 until the second measure, and several scales will allow us to do this. One scale that we can utilize—besides a scale to create altered tension—is some kind of scale that will give us primarily natural tension. A good scale for this would be the melodic minor scale a fifth higher than the root—in this case, a fifth higher than E is B, so we'll use a B melodic minor scale. (Remember: a B melodic minor scale is just a B major scale with a flatted 3rd.)

Phrase 3

In Phrase 3, the A7♭9 chord resolves to Dm7. The A7 functions as the V of Dm7, so I can use either natural or altered tension over the A7♭9 chord.

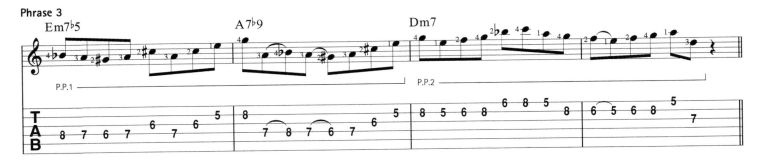

Practice Point 1: Over Em7♭5 to A7♭9, I play out of an A7 shape, emphasizing the ♭9 (B♭) and adding a chromatic lower neighbor (G♯). So I'm using mostly natural tension.

Practice Point 2: Over Dm7, the chord of resolution, I stay in the same position and play out of a D natural minor scale.

To bring out the sound of a natural dominant seventh chord, you have various options. You could use a melodic minor scale a fifth higher than A, which would be the E melodic minor scale. Or, if you wanted a more 11th and 13th sound over that A7 chord, you could use a major scale or a major seventh arpeggio a whole step down (e.g., Gmaj7).

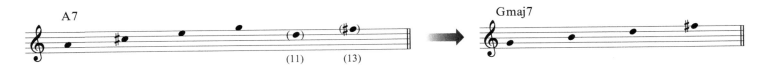

This is a favorite technique of Pat Martino and George Benson.

You could also use the key center that the dominant seventh chord comes from. Since A7 is the V in the key of D major, you could play a D major scale. If you played a D major scale starting on an A7 chord or on the root of A, you would actually be playing an A Mixolydian mode, and that works well over an A7♭9 chord. These are just some of the colors available to you here.

Tips for Strong Resolutions

Another important concept when improvising is *resolution*. When you're soloing over a chord and you reach the next chord, you must resolve properly. This means you must choose a note of the new chord that will lead the listener smoothly from the preceding chord. You should strive to move only a half step, either lower or higher, to get to a chord tone of the next scale. This makes for an uninterrupted line and a smooth resolution.

The next thing to strive for is to bring out the sound of the chord you are resolving to. This is accomplished by choosing a strong chord tone. Wes Montgomery, Pat Martino, and George Benson all had very, very strong chord tones in their resolutions.

A lot of players think that the root note of a chord is the best resolution tone, but the root is actually one of the weaker tones. You can use it, but the strongest tones to resolve to are the *fifth* of the chord, followed by the *third*. The third and fifth work well over major, dominant, and minor chords (use the minor third over a minor chord). Another strong tone is the *ninth*. Tones to avoid—the weaker tones—are the sixth, the flatted-seventh, the major seventh, and, again, the root.

Phrase 4

Now we come to our B section. Several things happen in this phrase over the E7♭9 chord. We can use altered tension over this chord, utilizing some of the scales previously suggested. One thing you'll hear in my solo is the use of a harmonic minor scale.

Practice Point 1: Since E7 is the V of A minor, what I play over the E7♭9 chord is an A harmonic minor scale. This works because a dominant seventh chord with a flatted 9th is part of the scale step harmony of the harmonic minor scale.

Practice Point 2: When I get to the Am chord, I start on the 9th (B), one of the strong resolution tones I mentioned earlier.

Phrase 5

Phrase 5 is another dominant seventh chord, D7. Since it's followed by another ii–V progression (Dm7–G7), it's a functioning dominant seventh.

When the Chords Go By Too Fast

Sometimes when soloing, we encounter chords that are moving by very quickly—as opposed to having one chord change per bar, we end up with two chords per bar. This creates a problem for the soloist because the chords are moving too fast. When this is the case, chances are good you're looking at a series of ii–V–I progressions.

So, what do we do to solve this problem? We change our thinking. When the chords are changing every two beats, instead of playing over the ii chord for the first two beats, and then the V chord for beats 3 and 4, we play over both chords as if we were playing only over the ii chord for all four beats. We can do this because there's an interesting plurality that exists between these chords. If the ii chord is Dm and the V chord is G7, it just so happens that the Dm6 arpeggio has nearly all the same notes as the G9 chord. So, because of that, we can play just over the ii chord.

George Benson and Pat Martino are really good at dealing with chord changes that happen very fast, and this is one of the techniques that help them cover these quick changes. When they see Dm for two beats, then G7 for two beats, they just play over Dm for four beats.

When I run into a series of these short progressions where I have ii–V after ii–V, I'll play over each of the ii chords as if the V chord wasn't there. For instance, if I see Dm7–G7–Em7–A7, I play D minor phrases and then E minor phrases, and I don't worry about the G7 or the A7.

Eventually, though, the series of ii–V chord changes will probably resolve to a I chord. When I see a series of ii–V changes leading eventually to a ii–V–I change, I play over each of the ii chords as it arrives, then on the very last ii–V–I, I might actually skip the ii chord altogether and just play phrases based on the V chord. In fact, I'll probably play altered tension type lines here.

This works because that final V chord serves as a functioning dominant seventh chord, which is an ideal place to use altered tension. This helps draw the listener to the point of resolution, the I chord. Setting up this tension, then resolving it on the final V–I cadence, is a very important concept.

Phrase 6

In Phrase 6, we move on to Dm and G7, a classic ii–V progression that leads us back to the return of the A section in the next phrase. Again, the G7 is a functioning dominant seventh because it will resolve to the tonic C chord.

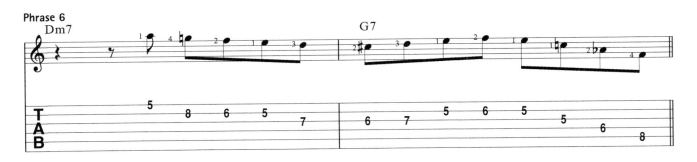

Phrase 7

The C chord at the start of this phrase resolves a series of V–I changes that began in our B section—with E7 moving to Am, then D7 moving to G7. Now the G7 resolves to C, the home key of the song. Notice the note of resolution, E, the 3rd of the C chord.

Phrase 8

With Phrase 8, we have E7 again, a functioning dominant seventh chord.

Phrase 9

In Phrase 9, we have another A7 chord resolving to Dm7. Notice the note of resolution at the start of the Dm7 chord.

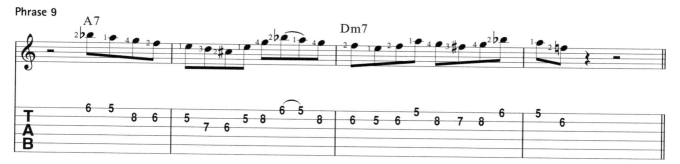

Phrase 10

The progression from F to F#°7 begins our last section and sets up the song's final turnaround.

Also, I want to point out that it helps give your solos more life—a little breath or airiness—when you start your patterns and ideas on the "and" of a beat, as opposed to on the downbeat. You'll notice I've done that here.

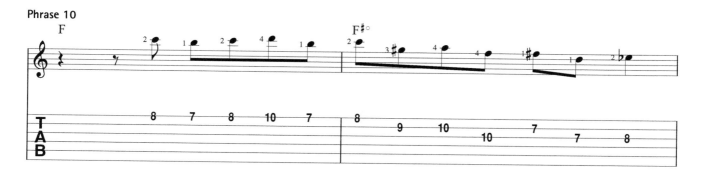

Phrase 11

Now I'm setting up the final bars of the song. The C and A7 chords kick off a classic I–VI–II–V–I jazz turnaround that culminates in the final D7–G7–C progression in Phrase 12.

Notice also that I answer the question posed in the previous phrase—repeating my idea exactly over the C chord, and raising it a half step over the A7 chord.

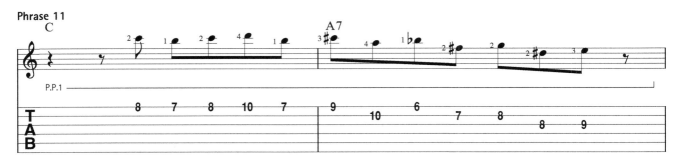

Phrase 12

This final II–V–I wraps up the song. The bass takes over on the C chord and begins its own solo.

The Mysterious Whole Tone Scale

Another very important tool in our study of tension and resolution, and something that Pat Martino favors, is the *whole tone scale.* This is a very unique and important scale we can utilize when improvising, especially over dominant seventh chords and altered dominant chords.

The whole tone scale in its entirety—usually one or two octaves—requires a lot of unusual fingering, and many guitar players shy away from this scale for that reason. But I'm going to show you a little trick that will make playing and using the whole tone scale easy.

The whole tone scale is just as the name suggests—all whole tones, or whole steps. The whole tone scale built on G, for example, includes the notes G, A, B, C♯, D♯, F, and G. But to make it easy and useful, we're only going to play a fragment of the scale.

We're going to stop here and not play the remaining two notes in the first octave of the scale (F and G) because the fingering is difficult, requiring you to shift your hand. So we're only going to play these five notes—and you can see that this fragment of a whole tone scale almost resembles a pentatonic scale.

G minor pentatonic

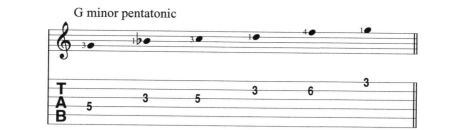

Now, because the whole tone scale is what's known as a symmetrical scale—in this case, made up of all whole steps—our fragment can be moved up and down the neck by whole step (two frets) and played exactly the same way. This stretches the pattern's usefulness, and covers any notes not reached in the abbreviated fingering.

The G whole tone scale will fit a G7 chord with a #5 or a ♭5, plus it has all the other tones that are in the G7 or the G9 chord. And you can mix this whole tone device up with different scale patterns, especially the altered tension patterns we've discussed in this chapter. This is something Pat Martino favors and, because it's very easy to play, he plays it fairly rapidly.

You could also employ the whole tone scale over a dominant seventh chord that's static—in a fusion type of vamp on a G7, for example, you could alternate between G minor pentatonic and the G whole tone scale. So, again, it's a very powerful tool, along with our others, for improvising.

The Final Resolution

I've covered a lot of material in this chapter, and I hope you can put it to use. I would also like to make a few suggestions that will help you to become the musician you want to be. First, I think you should play along with jazz records by famous jazz musicians. Put on any record and play along with it using your ears to guide you. Try to imitate their sound or ideas. Pick out several notes or phrases you like and try to instantly play it back. Then pick another phrase, and keep this up throughout the entire track. You'll be amazed at what you'll hear after repeated attempts.

Also, you should put together some kind of favorite licks book that has patterns like ii–V–I's, major ideas, minor ideas, and dominant ideas. You can collect these either by learning them from your favorite jazz recording artists, or making up some of your own.

I would also suggest that you get some transcriptions, find the ii–V–I's inside of them, and analyze them to see whether there's altered or natural tension being used over the V chord.

Also, look to see what note the last note of the V chord resolves to on the downbeat of the I chord. Is it the 5th of the I chord? The 3rd? Some other chord tone? This is another very important concept. You should become very aware of the resolution tendencies of your favorite artists.

I hope you enjoyed all of this. Good luck!

6

4 Jazz Blues

The blues is a very exciting musical style and something every jazz player should have together. All the great players—Wes Montgomery, Tal Farlow, Jimmy Raney, Barney Kessel, Herb Ellis, Joe Pass, and George Benson—are, or were, really proficient at playing the blues. And so, in order for us to develop as jazz players, we must understand the blues and some of the devices used to play it.

In this chapter, we'll learn three types of blues: 1) the traditional 12-bar blues as used in jazz, 2) a variation on this called the West Coast blues, and 3) the minor blues. My solo is in a traditional 12-bar jazz blues style—three times through the chorus. I'm not going to analyze the solo this time; I'll leave that to you. Instead, I'm going to discuss each of the aforementioned blues types—the types of blues you're likely to encounter as a jazz guitarist—explaining the chord substitutions as well as your various soloing options.

Jazz Blues

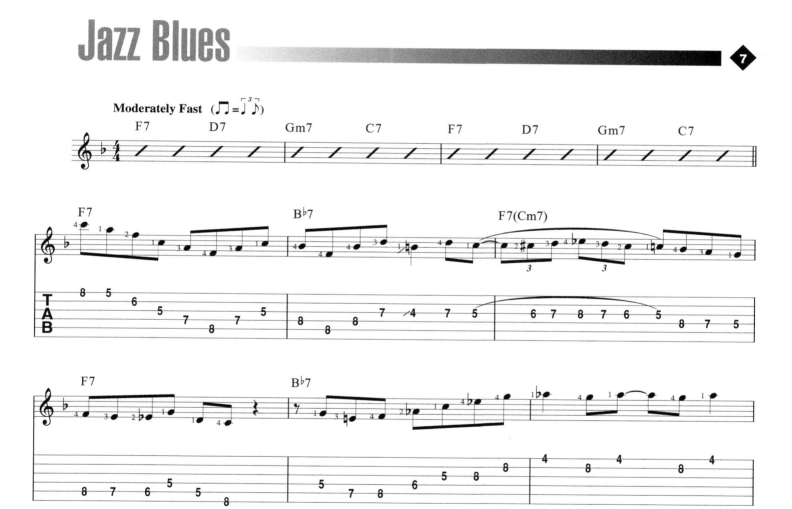

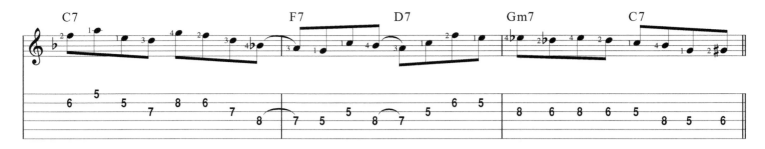

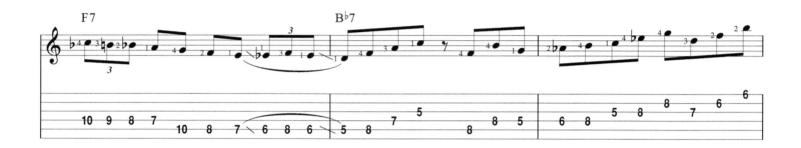

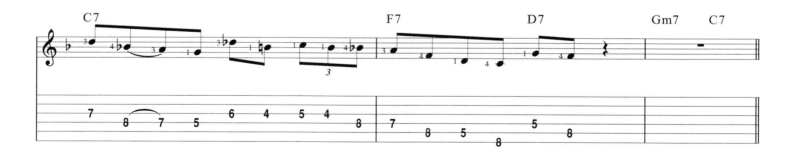

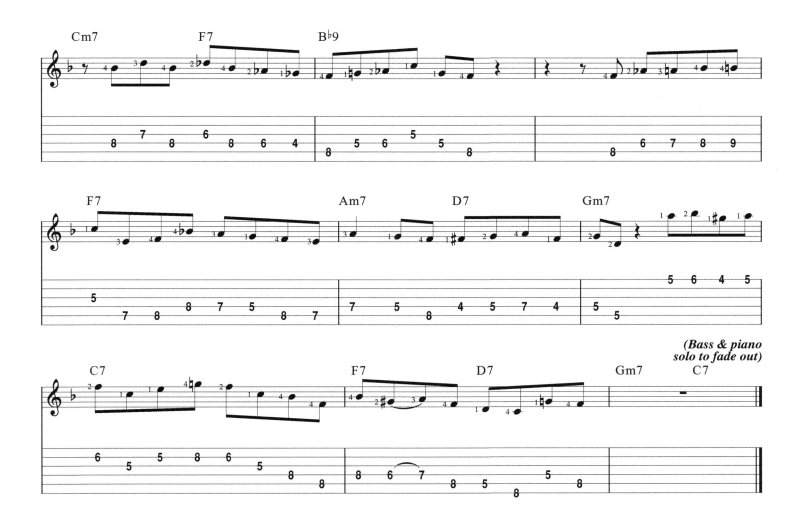

Traditional Jazz Blues

Most rock or pop guitar players understand playing the blues, but they look at blues as basically a I–IV–V progression. Before we get to how to approach soloing over a jazz blues, I'll show you the chordal variations a jazz player would make to a standard I–IV–V blues progression.

Let's use the key of F for example. Rock players will play an F minor pentatonic scale over a blues song in F, and they look at the progression as an F7 chord going up to a B♭7 chord, back to F7 again, and then to C and B♭7 and finishing on F7.

Standard 12-Bar Blues

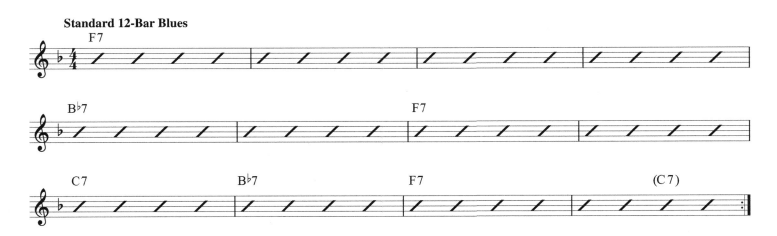

We're going to look at this progression a little differently. There are quite a few other chords that we want to add to this 12-bar blues, so pay attention.

8 ◆ A Typical 12-Bar Jazz Blues

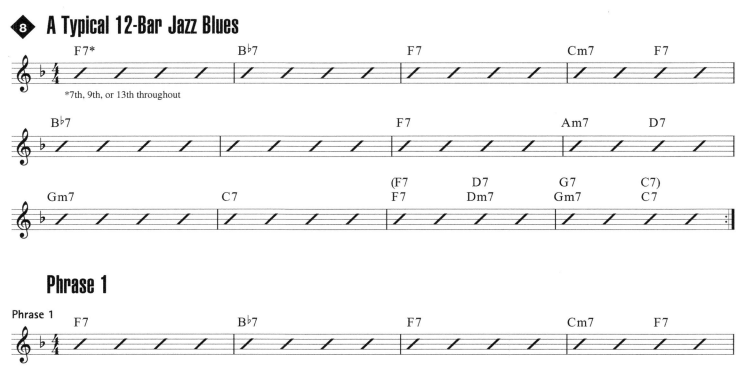

Phrase 1

To begin with, jazz players don't play dominant seventh chords that much—we usually add either the 9th or 13th to the chord. So in this progression, I would play F9 or F13, B♭9 or B♭13, and C9 or C13. Throughout this chapter—throughout this entire book, in fact—when I mention a chord such as F7, I'll mostly be referring to a dominant seventh chord in sort of a generic harmonic sense, but in its place I would almost always substitute a ninth or thirteenth chord. Wes Montgomery loved to play thirteenth chords instead of dominant seventh or even ninth chords.

So I might play F9 or F13 over the first three measures of the song. Alternatively, in the second measure, I might add what's called a *quick-change*, which means that I play the I chord in the first measure, then go to the IV chord in the second measure, then go back to the I chord for the third measure, as shown here. Quick-change progressions account for approximately 50 percent of all blues songs.

In the fourth measure, I'll do something different to set up the next phrase and to have a stronger resolution to the upcoming IV chord, B♭9 or B♭13. Since F is the V chord of B♭, what I'll do is put a minor chord in front of F to set up a ii–V moving to the B♭ chord. A ii–V change in the key of B♭ is Cm7–F7, so I'd play those two chords for two beats each in the fourth measure—or I might even stretch that out a little by playing Cm7 for the whole third measure, then F7 for the whole fourth measure.

Phrase 2

Phrase 2
B♭7   F7   Am7   D7

For the fifth and sixth measures, I stay on B♭7, just as in a standard 12-bar blues—though again, I'm more likely to play B♭9 or B♭13.

Then I make another change to the standard 12-bar blues progression. Normally in rock or traditional blues, the band will stay on the I chord, F7, in the seventh and eighth measures, before moving to the V chord, C7, in the next phrase. But in jazz, our third phrase will begin on a Gm7, the ii chord, and if possible, we'd like to set that chord up. So, what we'll do is play F7 (or F9 or F13) for the seventh measure, then in the eighth measure, we'll actually go to D7 (or D9 or D13). And in fact, to heighten that feeling, we may substitute two beats of Am and two beats of D7 in that eighth measure. Sometimes at this point, I'll play a D7 altered chord (D7♭5, D+7, D7♭9, etc.—remember, altered is the raising or lowering of the 5th or 9th).

Phrase 3

Again, as opposed to starting our third phrase on the V chord like a rock or blues player might, I'll go to the ii chord, Gm7. Then I go to C7, which I might play as a C9 chord, or it can be altered.

And then we reach the last two measures, the turnaround. In regular blues, the turnaround usually goes from the I chord to the V chord; in this key that would be F7 to C7. But in jazz, we usually use a I–vi–ii–V progression, so the turnaround would go F7–Dm7–Gm7–C7. Sometimes, a jazz player will make all four of the turnaround chords major (I–VI–II–V), so the progression might go F7–D7–G7–C7.

One More Substitution

That basic formula works in just about any jazz blues situation, but there are still a couple of other chords that we can add to this progression to spice it up even more.

In measures 7 and 8, not only can we go from F7 (or F9 or F13) to Am to D7, but we could also opt to just move F7 down by half steps. That means that we can play F7 or F13 for two beats, then move downward to E7 for two beats, then in the eighth measure, play E♭7 for two beats (instead of Am) and arrive at our D7.

So, we can move down chromatically: F for two beats, E for two beats, Eb for two beats, and then to our D7, which is a climax point of the blues.

And that's it. That's the basic formula for a jazz blues. I might play the progression through the first time without the chromatic movement just described, then the second time through add the chromatic changes in the seventh and eighth measures. And there are other chord substitutions I might make to vary the tune slightly each time through—if I were playing a solo gig without a band, for example, I might add a walking bass line to the chords the second time through to liven things up a little—but that's a book in itself. There are countless substitutions we could make to this basic jazz blues format, but let's get to soloing.

Soloing over a Jazz Blues

When improvising with the 12-bar blues, most jazz players will take the minor pentatonic scale as their starting point—in this case, we're in the key of F playing an F minor pentatonic—but they'll also make use of other scales.

Phrase 1

Practice Point 1: One common scale to use is a melodic minor scale a fifth higher than the root of the chord; this gives a different character to the blues. If I'm playing an F7 (or F9 or F13) chord, a fifth higher is C. So, when the band plays F7, I can play C melodic minor.

Practice Point 2: When the band goes to B♭7, I can make the same substitution and play a fifth higher than B♭—F melodic minor. However—and this is more likely—because this is a quick-change, I can also choose to disregard this chord and for the first three bars just solo over an F7 chord, playing out of the C melodic minor scale.

Practice Point 3: In the fourth measure of this 12-bar blues, we have Cm7 to F7, a ii–V progression leading into the B♭7 in the next phrase. I usually try to set up that B♭7 chord with an altered scale based on the V chord. I learned this from Wes Montgomery. One such scale would be the melodic minor a half step higher than the V chord. So if the band plays Cm7 to F7, I can play a melodic minor scale a half step higher than F over that whole measure—in other words, an F♯ or G♭ melodic minor scale.

Phrase 2

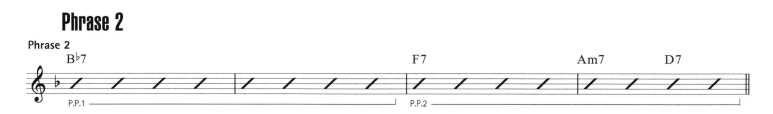

Practice Point 1: In the fifth and sixth measures of our 12-bar blues, I play over the IV chord, B♭7, using an F melodic minor scale.

Practice Point 2: In the seventh measure, over F7, I use the same substitute as at the top of the tune—the C melodic minor scale. Then I reach the climax point of the blues tune, the eighth measure. In this measure, we're on an Am7 going to D7, or the whole measure could be considered D7 altered. I really want to bring out the sound of this climax point, so I use an altered scale: the melodic minor a half step higher than D, E♭ melodic minor.

I choose an altered scale over D7 because it's the V of the chord we're going to in the next phrase, Gm7, and I want the listener to really hear that resolution. Wes Montgomery, Joe Pass, and all the great jazz guitar players will draw out the sound of the dominant seventh chord like this using altered tension. You can hear the same thing from all the legendary horn players—Charlie Parker, Sonny Rollins, John Coltrane.

Phrase 3

Practice Point 1: At this point in our 12-bar pattern, we have a ii–V progression: Gm7 to C7. For the C7 chord, I might play a C7 altered chord—either ♭5, ♯5, ♭9, or ♯9—or a plain old C9, C11, or C13 chord. It's during this time that we have the release on the tune. This is where we can play one of our favorite ii–V licks.

Practice Point 2: Now we come to the last two measures of the progression, the I–vi–ii–V turnaround. This is a very important point in the song because it leads us back to the top of the tune. We can do several things here. We can either play out of the F key center to satisfy the sound of this turnaround, or we can play over each individual chord, or we can do any conceivable combination of both of those approaches.

A lot of players, when they get to the last two measures of the blues—especially when they hit the I chord (F) at the start of the turnaround—will sort of let their solo down. They come out of the preceding ii–V–I (Gm7 to C7 to F7), and then they stop soloing and just play a more rhythm- or chord-oriented turnaround. But it's very important that you learn how to solo over turnarounds because you can use that as a launching pad *into* your solo, or into the *next chorus* of your solo.

When they finish one chorus of a tune, Joe Pass and other players will definitely use the turnaround as a launching pad to start the chorus over again, carrying their ideas through the turnaround and right into the very beginning of the next chorus. Then when they get to the I chord at the beginning of their next chorus, that's when they'll breathe or take a rest.

Another thing to consider is that there is more than one substitute for these turnaround chords. We learned earlier that we can substitute C melodic minor for F7. That's a really good sub. Another thing we can do is bring out the sound of an F13 chord, especially as we go from F7 to D7. D is the 6th or 13th of F, so playing an F13 sound over the F7 to D7 progression works well. To do this, we can use a major seventh arpeggio or a major scale a minor third higher than that original substitute, C melodic minor. A minor third higher than C minor is E♭ major, and E♭ major is a whole step lower than F7. So the rule is that when we see a dominant seventh chord and we want to bring out the sound of a ninth or thirteenth in its place, we simply play a maj7 (or maj9) arpeggio a whole step lower. That is a common substitute we can use.

And we can combine these approaches. When the band is playing F7, we can play C melodic minor, then switch to E♭ major. This is a typical thing George Benson and Pat Martino would do, and all the horn players use these devices as well. You can either use the simple arpeggios or you can combine everything together.

West Coast Blues

There is another form of the blues called the West Coast blues that I'd like to explain now. It adds a few variations to our regular jazz blues.

◆ The West Coast Jazz Blues

When improvising over the West Coast blues chord progression, we have a slight change in plans.

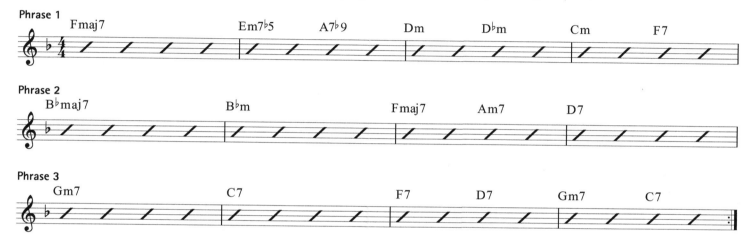

Phrase 1

Number one, for our first chord, Fmaj7, we play an F major scale. Then we have a minor ii–V progression: Em7♭5 to A7♭9. But since those chords are occurring for only two beats each, we can ignore the Em7♭5 and just play over A7♭9 for the whole measure. Then in the third and fourth measures, in place of the usual F7 or I chord of a 12-bar blues, we solo over Dm to D♭m, and then Cm to F7.

Phrase 2

In the fifth and sixth measures of the 12-bar blues, the usual chord would be IV7, in this case B♭7. But in the West Coast blues, we have B♭maj7 in the fifth measure, then B♭m in the sixth measure, and we solo over those. Then in the seventh measure, again in place of the usual F7, we have two possibilities: Fmaj7 or Am7. Then we play D7 or D7 altered—in this case D7♭9—for the eighth measure.

Phrase 3

The last four measures of the West Coast jazz blues are the same as the normal jazz blues, beginning with a ii–V (Gm7 to C7) and then moving to a I–VI–ii–V (F7–D7–Gm7–C7) turnaround.

That's a West Coast version of the blues. So, I've given you two types of blues here, or two jazzy variations on our standard 12-bar blues.

Minor Blues

There's another jazz blues variation I'd like you to be familiar with: the minor blues. The minor blues is just as the name suggests, primarily minor. Early commercial rock by artists such as Santana would make use of the minor blues, but it would be similar to a regular traditional blues—a I–IV–V progression—except the i and iv chords would be minor. In the key of C minor, for example, the chords would be Cm, Fm, and G7.

Once again, however, it's a little different when you're playing a jazz minor blues. I'll chart this song in the key of C minor.

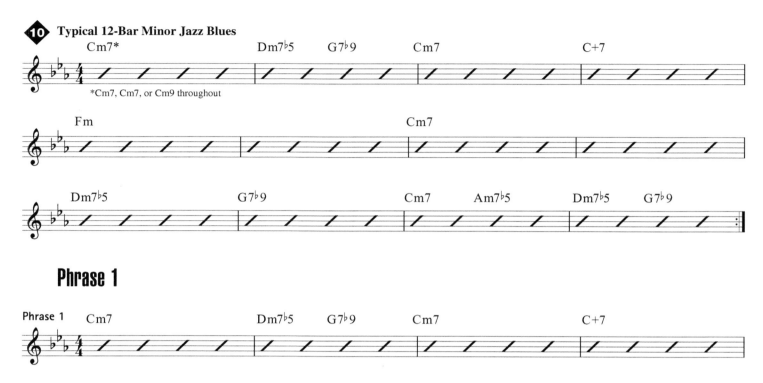

Phrase 1

In order to create interest for the listener on a minor blues, jazz players not only use a regular minor chord, they also use a 6th and 9th scale degree. The 6th degree of the Cm chord is an A, so I would play a Cm6 chord, or I would play a Cm9 chord using a D as the 9th. Those are common tones to add. Another color tone that jazz players also utilize is a major 7th (B) over a minor chord. Wes Montgomery loved to use the major seventh like this.

In the second measure, again to create more interest for the listener, I use Dm7♭5 for two beats to G7♭9 for two beats, because that's a ii–V going back to Cm. In the third measure, I go back to Cm. And then in the fourth measure, to set up the Fm chord in the following measure, we're going to play a C+7 chord. Even though we're playing a minor blues, we're going to draw the sound of that F minor out by playing C+7. This is the V of F minor, so we make a V-to-i move there, but there's another thing that works out well here. When playing C+7, the sharp 5 of C7 is a G♯ or, enharmonically, A♭. And A♭ happens to be the flatted 3rd of Fm. So, we can draw out the sound of that Fm chord by playing the C+7.

Phrase 2

We play F minor for two measures, and then we go back to Cm for two measures.

Phrase 3

In the ninth and tenth measures, we play a ii–V; in the key of C minor, that's Dm7♭5 to G7♭9 (or G+7, whatever we prefer). And then in final two measures, we have a minor turnaround. The minor turnaround is Cm7– Am7♭5– Dm7♭5–G7♭9.

Soloing Over a Minor Blues
Phrase 1

Practice Point 1: When improvising over the i chord in the key of C minor—the Cm chord—we can play a C melodic minor scale. That's a very common substitute. We could also use C Dorian or a C harmonic minor scale. A harmonic minor scale will give us a very strong sound, especially if we use it in the second measure.

Practice Point 2: For the second measure, because we have a minor ii–V progression—Dm7♭5 to G7♭9—we could play a C harmonic minor scale. So what we could do is this: in the first measure, improvise with the C melodic minor scale; in the second measure, go to the C harmonic minor scale; and then for the third measure, go back to C melodic minor.

Practice Point 3: In the fourth measure, we have our C7 altered chord, C+7, and we want to be careful with our C7 altered because we want to draw out the sound of that. We want to play some scale that will give us altered tension, as discussed in the previous chapter. So, what we're going to do here is use a C♯ melodic minor scale. This will lead us right to Fm in the fifth and sixth measures.

Phrase 2

Practice Point 1: During the Fm, of course, we can utilize an F melodic minor scale or any other combination, like F harmonic minor.

Practice Point 2: Then we go back to Cm and the C melodic minor scale again in the seventh and eighth measures.

Phrase 3

Practice Point 1: Then from there, we encounter Dm7♭5 to G7♭9 in the ninth and tenth measures. For that, we can use a C harmonic minor scale.

Practice Point 2: And then we come to the turnaround: Cm7–Am7♭5–Dm7♭5–G7♭9. This is a typical jazz I–vi–ii–V turnaround, except that the I chord is minor (i). During that turnaround, since all these chords belong to either the C harmonic or C melodic minor scale, we could play either one of those scales.

Another thing to understand here is that the second chord in the turnaround—the vi chord, Am7♭5—is, enharmonically, the same as a Cm6 chord. Knowing this, the progression becomes Cm7 to Cm6, which allows us to just play a C minor scale, either melodic minor or harmonic minor, for the first measure of the turnaround. Then, when we come to our Dm7♭5 to G7♭9, we can also play the harmonic minor scale. So, this means, again, that we can play a harmonic minor scale for all of the chords in the turnaround.

One More Cool Soloing Device

Another device that we can utilize when improvising over this minor blues—or over any song in any key for that matter—is to play scales in vertical fashion.

When we play a scale one note after the other, that's horizontal, but we can also play a scale *vertically*. In other words, we take the scale, harmonize it, and play the resulting arpeggios. In this case, for a minor jazz blues in C, we'll use a C harmonic minor scale.

Arpeggios of the Harmonic Minor Scale

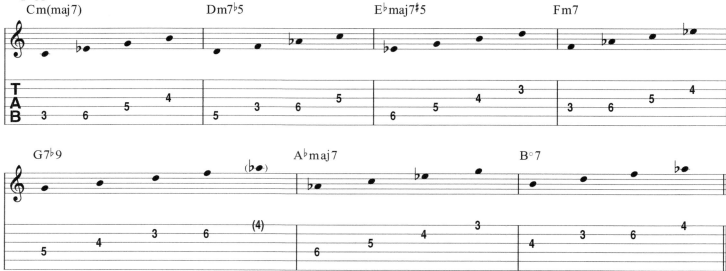

Now, if we play all of these arpeggios one after the other, we're really just playing the C harmonic minor scale, aren't we? But we're playing the arpeggios that make up the scale, so it sounds vertical and different for the listener.

So, this is a device that you can utilize, but you don't have to play all of the arpeggios—let's try playing every other one. Start with Cm(maj7), then skip to E♭maj7♯5, then to G7♭9, then to B°7.

Solo Using Arpeggios of the Harmonic Minor Scale

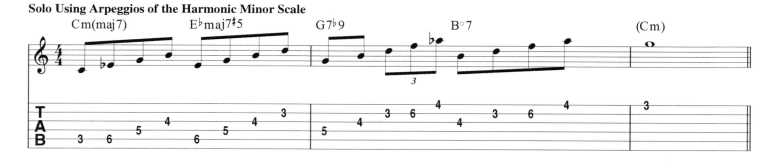

This is a typical device that George Benson utilizes. Often, when he encounters a minor ii–V–i progression, he plays a verticalization of a harmonic minor scale. So, this is a very common solo technique to utilize, and you can do this with other scales as well.

Blues You Can Use

In this chapter, we've covered playing the 12-bar jazz blues three different ways: the regular jazz blues variation on the standard 12-bar rock 'n' roll blues, the West Coast version of the jazz blues, and the minor jazz blues.

After awhile, you'll be able to hear the West Coast version so distinctively that, cycling through chord progressions, you'll be able to pick up on it right away. So, when your friends start playing it, you'll just hear it and go, "Oh, they're moving through the West Coast progression," and you can jam over it. You should learn how to improvise through both of those, and also be equipped to improvise on the minor blues. With those three, you'll have covered all the basic jazz blues styles.

Another thing I would suggest for guitar players is to learn how to play the blues in the key of F. A lot of guitar players learn it in the key of B♭ or C, when a lot of keyboard players play in the key of F instead. In doing so, don't get stuck playing F pentatonic riffs at the 1st or 13th fret. In this book, we've covered substitutes that you can apply to this to get yourself out of that pentatonic rut, including playing the C melodic minor scale and the E♭maj7 arpeggio or scale over the F7 chord. So, by switching between the E♭maj7, the F minor pentatonic scale, and the C melodic minor scale, we cover a lot of melodic ground, and the whole fingerboard is filled in and just becomes one.

I hope you've had a wonderful time with this jazz blues chapter. I hope I've inspired you to work with it, listen to records by your favorite jazz players, and get into playing the blues.

5 Chord Soloing

I n this chapter, I'll show you a little about soloing with chords. This is something Barney Kessel, Kenny Burrell, Wes Montgomery, Ed Bickert, and other guitar players have been doing for years. It's an incredible technique because, when you're soloing on the guitar with single notes, being able to come in and suddenly start soloing with chords will give your playing an extra dimension, a fuller harmonic texture. There are a lot of different techniques and tricks we can utilize for this, and I'll discuss them in this chapter.

In a sense, when chord soloing, the guitar acts like a miniature big band, and one place to find inspiration for this style of soloing is big band records. The horn section harmonizes melodies just as we do when we solo with chords; you can pick up a lot of tips by just listening to them.

My solo here is over a 12-bar blues in F. Rather than trying to copy it, just listen to it to get a sense of the style, and then I'll explain how to approach this type of playing.

Harmonizing a Melody

The first thing that we must learn how to do is to actually harmonize a melody or a lick. Let's take a ii–V–I progression for instance: Am–D7–Gmaj7. I'd recommend that you record these chord changes, playing four beats each. Once you've recorded the chord changes, the next step is to play a melody over those changes—just a simple melody, something you can come up with using the notes of those chords. Then, we'll harmonize it, and this will get us into soloing with chords.

When we harmonize a melody, what we actually do is take a note—one of the tones in a particular chord that we're playing—and make it the top note of the chord, whatever it is. Let's say we have a melody over Am, and the notes are E and B. So we say to ourselves, "What is an E to an Am chord?" It's the 5th. So, what we do is we look for some kind of Am chord that has E on top—E as the highest note in the chord. Then the next note is B. What is B to an Am chord? It's the 9th. So, do we know any Am9 chords with the 9th on top? (When I refer to top, I mean the highest-pitched string.)

How do we go about finding chords like this? The first thing you do is go through any chord dictionaries you have, any kind of chord books whatsoever, and you look for all the major chords first. You look for the top note—the note that's highest in pitch in whatever chord voicing you're looking at. Let's say you had a group of C chords and on top of a particular Cmaj7 chord there is an E note—the highest note in the chord voicing.

Take a red pen and mark "3rd" because E is the 3rd of C major. You do that with minor chords, too. You find a minor chord with a 3rd on top, let's say an Am chord with a C on top. An Am chord with a 5th on top, which is E; with the 9th, B; with the root on top—A. And you mark this down in your book. And you fill the entire book up with these little red markings.

So, by marking up this dictionary, we take a regular chord book—a lot of voicings we wouldn't even think of using—and we turn it into a very powerful tool. Because we've marked the 3rd on top, the 5th, the 9th, the ♭9, the ♯9, etc. on every chord. And by doing that, we're in a very powerful position; we can just open the book up and harmonize any melody. This can become a very effective tool for us. Once you have your book, you can take a chord progression and record a melody over it, and then you can practice developing your ideas.

Chord Soloing Techniques

Phrase 1: Harmonizing Chord Tones

When it comes time to harmonize a solo, you sit down and take a chord progression and play a little melody over it. For this example, playing the chords Am7–D7–Gmaj7, let's use the melody notes E, B, E♭, B♭, A, and we'll harmonize that.

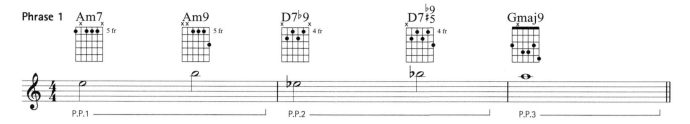

Practice Point 1: So, we say to ourselves, "What is the first chord we're playing?" We're playing an Am7 chord with an E on top, then an Am9 with a B on top.

Practice Point 2: Then, we have a D7 chord with an E♭, which is a flatted 9th, making a D7♭9 chord. Then we play a D7 chord with a B♭, or, enharmonically, A♯, which is a D7♭9♯5 chord.

Practice Point 3: And then we have an A note with a G chord, which is the 9th. So, we look for a G chord with a 9th on top, and play a Gmaj9 chord.

Phrase 2: Harmonizing Non-Chord Tones

The technique described in Phrase 1 works well for harmonizing chord tones, but there are other tones that we run into besides chord tones—non-chord tones—and we need to be able to harmonize those as well.

Non-chord tones are tones that aren't in the chord. That means if we have a Cmaj7 chord and the lick that you want to harmonize with that—an E, an F, and a G—you have to find a way to harmonize any notes in that lick that aren't in the chord. So, you look in your book and you say, "OK, E is the 3rd of C." Then you look in your book and say, "F is the fourth of C," and you don't have any chords like that. So you say to yourself, "This is a non-chord tone." You look farther into the lick and you see that the G note is the 5th of C, so you can play a Cmaj7 chord with G on top.

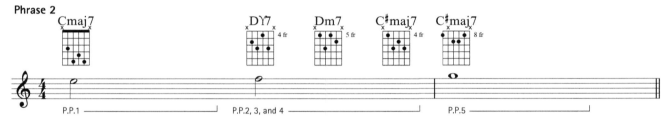

Practice Point 1: Play a Cmaj7 with E on top.

Practice Point 2: Here we have the F note. So what do we do with the non-chord tone F? The first thing we do is to try to use some chord that belongs to more than one key area. And the chord we will utilize in this example is a diminished chord.

The diminished chord is a very powerful chord. It belongs to at least three different key centers and because of that it doesn't really have one key area or one identity. So, we can utilize this in a lick where the band is playing a C chord but we're playing an E, F, and a G note for the melody. To harmonize that F note, we would utilize a diminished chord with F as the top note, in this case a D diminished chord. This is one way of dealing with a non-chord tone like this.

Practice Point 3: Another way to harmonize this non-chord tone is this: Because this F note isn't in the C major chord, but it is part of a C major scale, I can use another chord from the C scale step harmony. The C scale step harmony—building chords using only scale tones on each step of the scale—is C, Dm, Em, F, G7, Am, Bm7♭5, and back to C again.

So, I could say to myself, "Do any of these other chords in the C harmonized major scale have an F note, and particularly, do they have an F note on top in this area of the neck?" Yes, there are several chords. One such chord would be a Dm chord, the ii chord. So I could harmonize our E note with a C major chord, then I could move up and harmonize the F note with the Dm chord, and then harmonize the G note with a C major chord again.

Practice Point 4: Now, another thing that I could do is slide the C chord. That means that I could play a C chord with an E on top, then slide it up to C♯ and catch the F note, which is on top of the C♯maj7.

Practice Point 5: And then I can play a G note on top of a Cmaj7 chord to finish the melody.

Phrase 3: More Uses for the Diminished Chord

Guitar melodies often include chromatic notes, notes that you normally wouldn't have in a regular melody. Because these notes are not in the chord and sometimes not even in the scale of the key center, we need to find some chord to harmonize them. The diminished chord is a great tool for this. We can utilize it many places.

Wes Montgomery would use chromatic notes regularly and he would often harmonize them with a diminished chord. In fact, Wes would even use a diminished chord over notes that were part of the regular chord.

In Phrase 3a we'll play a diatonic melody—a melody using only notes from the A minor scale: A, B, C, D, and E. We'll harmonize that melody using nothing but variations on an A minor chord. In Phrase 3b we'll play the same melody the way Wes Montgomery might have played it, using diminished chords in place of some of the Am voicings.

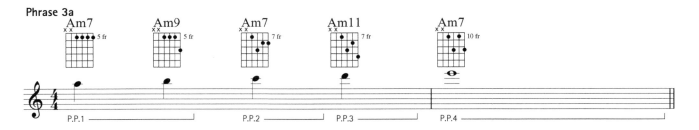

Practice Point 1: For the melody notes A and B, let's play an Am7 chord at the 5th fret with an A on top, and then add a B at the 7th fret to it to make Am9.

Practice Point 2: And then for the C melody note, play Am7 at the 7th fret: A at the 7th fret on the fourth string with your first finger, E at the 9th fret on the third string with your third finger, G at the 8th fret on the second string with your second finger, and then lay your second finger down to also catch the C note at the 8th fret on the first string.

Practice Point 3: For the D melody note, play Am11. It's the same chord as the previous Am7, but with your little finger reaching up to play D at the 10th fret on the first string.

Practice Point 4: For the E melody note, use this Am7 voicing: Play C at the 10th fret on the fourth string with your first finger. Barre that finger across the top four strings. Play G at the 12th fret on the third string with your third finger, A at the 10th fret on the second string with your first finger barre, and E at the 12th fret on the first string with your fourth finger.

This Am7 with an E on top was one of Wes Montgomery's favorite voicings.

Phrase 3b

Now let's use Wes Montgomery's technique of substituting diminished chords for some of those Am voicings. Wes particularly liked to sub a diminished chord for a ninth chord.

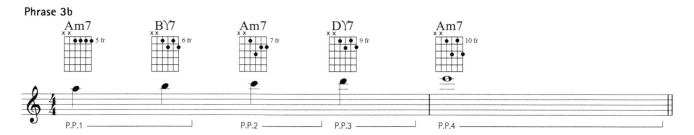

Practice Point 1: For the A melody note, play an Am7 chord by barring the top four strings at the 5th fret with your first finger.

Practice Point 2: For the B melody note, play a B°7 chord with a B on top.

Practice Point 3: For the C melody note, play the Am7 chord at the 7th fret.

Practice Point 4: For the D melody note, play a D°7 chord with a D on top.

Practice Point 5: For the E melody note, play the Am7 chord at the 10th fret.

Phrase 4: Sliding Chord Shapes

Wes also liked to slide into his chords—e.g., from a half step below or above. You can really cover a lot of melodic ground this way, using one or two chord shapes and sliding them up and down by half step. This is where things can get chromatic.

Phrase 4

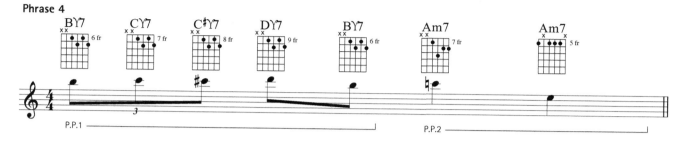

Practice Point 1: Play a B°7 chord with a B on top. Then slide it up one fret to play C°7 with C on top; then up another fret to play a C#°7 chord with a C# on top; then up another fret to play D°7 with D on top. Then move the shape back down to the original B°7.

Practice Point 2: Play Am7 with C on top, and Am7 with E on top.

Actually, you could slide any of these chord shapes up or down—including the minor sevenths. Feel free to experiment with this.

When Should I Harmonize?

One of the most important things when harmonizing a melody is to understand that we do not have to harmonize every note. So, when we attempt to harmonize melodies we have all kinds of options.

Let's say we had a triplet and the triplet consists of E, G, and A played over a C chord, and we're trying to figure out what notes to harmonize. There are several possibilities.

For one, when we come to that section of the tune, we don't have to harmonize any of those notes if we don't want to. We could just simply play the three notes and harmonize another part of the tune. Or, we might want to harmonize all three with triads, with each note ending up on top of a triad.

We might want to harmonize the first note of the triplet, play the second note by itself, and then harmonize the third note. We may want to play the first two notes and then harmonize the last note. So those are possibilities too.

And we don't have to use full chords—we can use thirds or other intervals to harmonize the melody. We can use sixths, or octaves, with the melody notes on top of each interval. When we use two-part chords or intervals such as thirds, sixths, or octaves, that's called two-part density. When we use triads, it's three-part density; with four-note chords, it's four-part density.

So, you must understand that we don't have to harmonize every note. The main thing is to keep the chords simple, using primarily major sevenths, minor sevenths, or dominant sevenths. And use a lot of half-step approaches: one half step, two half steps, three half steps. There are a lot of possibilities opened up for us.

Phrase 5: A Lead-In Note

When soloing with chords, we run into other problems besides just triplets. Sometimes, we run into a lead-in note, a non-chord tone that starts off the lick. Let's say we have a C chord, but the lick we play over it is a triplet figure—E to G to A—beginning with a chromatic lead-in note: D#. We can do several things in this situation.

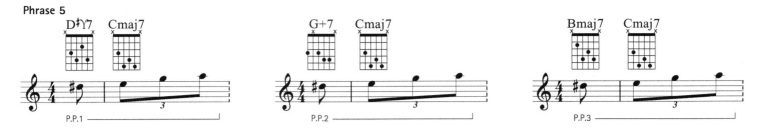

Practice Point 1: We can use a diminished chord for the D♯ note, resolving to the C chord for the E note (then playing G and A as single notes).

Practice Point 2: We could ask ourselves, "What's the strongest chord that will resolve to a C chord?" This happens to be a G7 chord, the V of C. In a G7 chord, D♯ is not a natural chord tone, but it is a ♯5. So we could play an altered G7—G+7 resolving to the C chord (again, playing G and A as single notes).

Practice Point 3: We could half-step approach the C chord with a B chord, then resolve as usual.

Phrase 6: Sweeping the Chords

Now, another technique that's utilized when soloing with chords—one used by Barney Kessel, especially—is a sweeping of the chords. Barney will take a series of chords and sweep across them—digging in with his pick to sound each note individually, but still essentially strumming them.

For this example in the key of G major, we'll play the descending melody D, C, B, A, A♭, G♭, F, E♭, D.

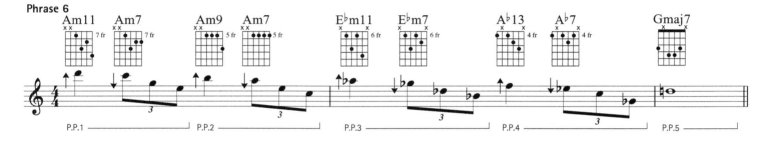

Practice Point 1: To play the D melody note, hold the Am11 chord and sweep across the strings, using a long, slow downstroke of the pick. Then, to play the C melody note (or the triplet figure), hold the Am7 chord and sweep across the strings in the opposite direction, using a long, slow upstroke.

Practice Point 2: To play the B melody note, hold the Am9 chord, and sweep across the strings with a slow downstroke. Then, to play the A melody note (or the triplet figure), hold the Am7 chord and sweep across the strings with a slow upstroke.

Practice Point 3: To play the A♭ melody note, hold the E♭m11 chord and sweep across the strings using a slow downstroke. Then, to play the G♭ melody note (or the triplet figure), hold the E♭m7 chord and sweep across the strings using a slow upstroke.

Practice Point 4: To play the F melody note, hold the A♭13 chord and sweep across the strings with a slow downstroke. Then, to play the E♭ melody note (or the triplet figure), hold the A♭7 chord and sweep across the strings using a slow upstroke.

Practice Point 5: To play the D melody note, resolve to a Gmaj7 chord.

Phrase 7: Melodies and Chords

There are other ways of soloing with chords. Sometimes, we can play little melodies on top while sounding another chord in the bottom. This simulates a pianistic approach, where you have a melody played by one hand and chord accompaniment played by the other.

Let's use the following melody as an example, over the chord progression Am7–D13–Gmaj9–E7#9. We'll also slide into the Am7 chord from a half step above. Sliding in from a half step above or below the chord adds to the pianistic effect.

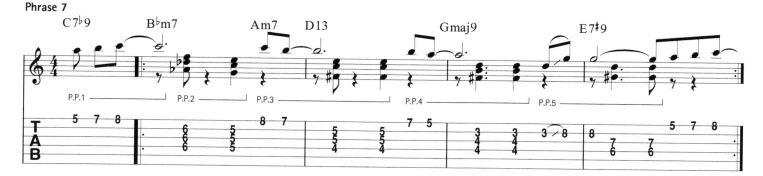

Practice Point 1: Play the melody notes as a single-note line: A, B, C. Let the C note ring.

Practice Point 2: While still holding the C melody note, play a B♭m7 chord, using a first-finger barre. Pluck these notes simultaneously with either fingers or hybrid picking (fingers and pick). Then, with the C note still ringing, move the first finger barre down one fret to play Am7.

Practice Point 3: Play the melody notes C and B, holding the B. Play the D13 chord. (Actually, the chord we play is a D9, but the B melody note makes it a D13).

Practice Point 4: Play the melody notes B and A. Then, holding the A note, play the Gmaj9 voicing below it. (Again, this is a Gmaj7 chord, but the A makes it a Gmaj9.)

Practice Point 5: Play the melody note D sliding up to G, then fill out the rest of the E7#9 chord.

Phrase 8: Chord Fragments

Another thing we can do is utilize fragments of chords. Ed Bickert is a guitarist who uses this a lot; he'll take a chord like Em7, play the top note and let it ring, and then play the rest of the chord, or part of it, below that, in rhythm.

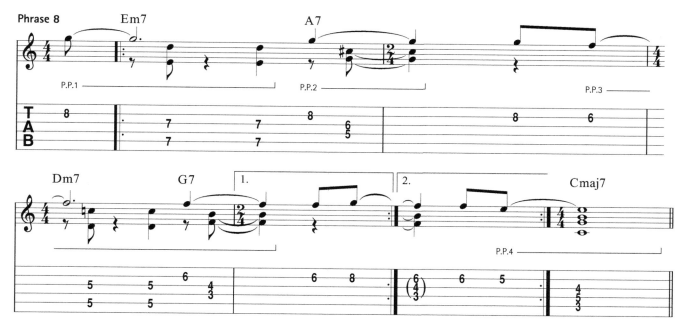

Practice Point 1: Play the G note of the Em7 with your little finger, and let it ring, then play the root (E) and flatted 7th (D).

Practice Point 2: Keeping your pinky on the G, strike the note again and then play A7, using the 7th (G) and 3rd (C#).

Practice Point 3: Repeat this idea one whole step (two frets) down. Play the F note of Dm7 with your little finger, let it ring, and play the root (D) and flatted 7th (C). Then play G7, using the 7th (F) and 3rd (B).

Practice Point 4: Resolve to a Cmaj7 chord.

Phrase 9: Pivoting around an Altered Note

Another thing that players like Ed Bickert will do—and Jim Hall, for that matter—is, if they're playing an altered chord, such as Em7♭5, they'll take the most important note of the chord, the altered note (the flat 5th, in this case) and pivot around it. Then they'll play the other notes of the chord underneath.

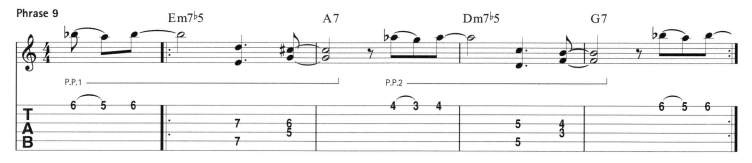

Practice Point 1: The ♭5 of Em7♭5 is the note B♭, so play that note, pull off to the note a half step below, then play B♭ again. Then play the other notes of the chord: E and D. Then go to an A7 chord, but playing only the 3rd (C♯) and 7th (G).

Practice Point 2: Repeat this idea one whole step (two frets) down, over Dm7♭5 to G7.

Concluding Our Chord Chemistry

If you listen to players such as Ed Bickert, Jim Hall, Barney Kessel, and Wes Montgomery, you'll notice that each of them has his own unique style. And each player has certain types of voicings that he prefers over other types of chord voicings.

But you don't have to solo just with harmonized chords. You can solo with single notes or with double stops or intervals, such as thirds, sixths, or octaves. Mixing all of these techniques will create interest for the listener. And you can put these techniques to use in different configurations. Wes Montgomery would usually solo with single notes first, then he would solo with octaves, and then with chords. Some players will solo with octaves first, then single notes, then chords—or just single notes then chords. Barney Kessel prefers to solo with single notes and then he'll go into soloing with chords.

Now that you understand how to harmonize melodies into chord solos, you can play with the recorded rhythm section and do your own chord soloing. The rhythm-only track is a blues tune in F. The blues is a great place to start to learn how to solo with chords. Make up your own melodies or licks for this tune and harmonize them; or just try using different chord voicings to create little melodies on the spot.

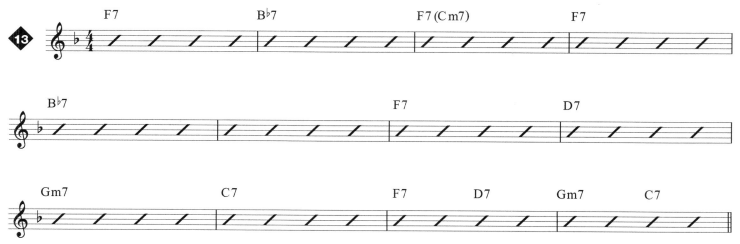

F7   B♭7   F7 (Cm7)   F7

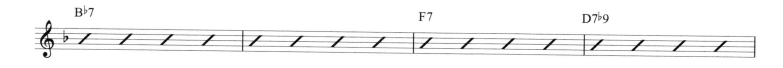

B♭7   F7   D7♭9

Gm7   C7   F7   D7   Gm7   C7

F13   B♭9   F7   Cm7   F7

B♭9   F7   Am7   D7

Gm7   C7   F   D7   Gm7   C7

6 Virtuoso Guitar

In this chapter, I cover a style of playing that I call "virtuoso guitar." This is the musical style played by such artists as Joe Pass and Barney Kessel. Virtuoso guitar involves the use of melody and solo or chordal fills. A lot of times you'll hear a guitarist play a melody to a song and then, in between the melody phrases of the song, you'll hear them fill in with these incredible jazz licks or chordal passages. This is virtuoso guitar playing.

In classical music, virtuosity refers to musical passages played by artists who have a lot of technique on their instrument. In this chapter, I'll explain some of the tools and approaches we can utilize to play in this style. So let's get into it.

Virtuoso Guitar

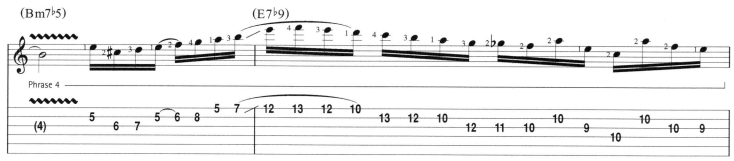

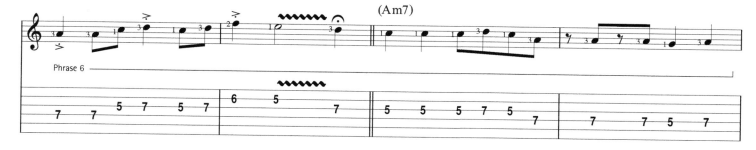

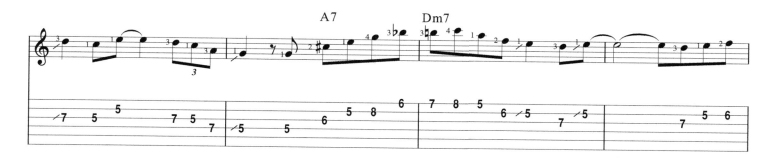

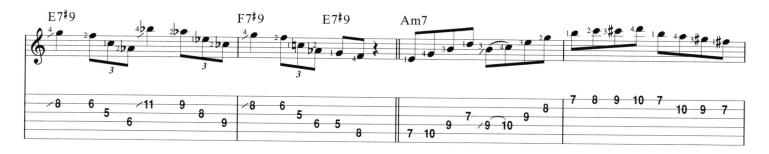

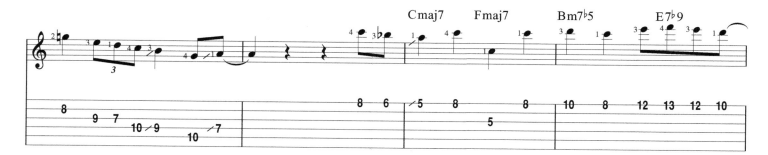

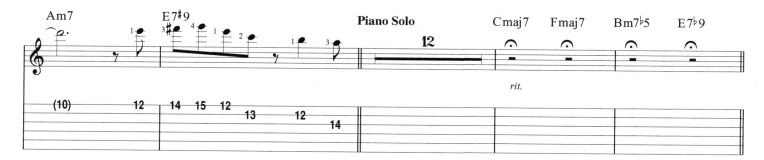

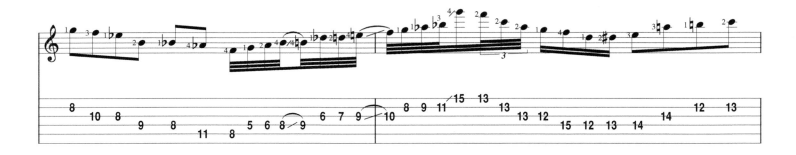

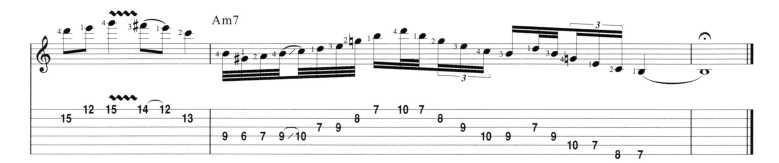

The Solo

The first thing that we're going to deal with in virtuoso guitar is the use of melody and fills. This can create a lot of interest for the listener, especially if you begin a song by playing the melody to the tune—or harmonizing the melody to the tune—*out of tempo*. A lot of times, as opposed to starting a tune in tempo, we play an introduction to a tune at a slower tempo, and then after a few measures of introduction, we start playing the song in tempo. We usually start by playing a small section of the melody and then, when the melody is at rest, we play some kind of fill. We repeat this a few times, and then we go into the song itself, at tempo.

The first several phrases of my solo "Virtuoso Guitar" are played *rubato*, or at a tempo that suits the mood of the player, without regard for consistent time. In rubato playing, some of the notes' tempo values may be stretched—a quarter note may be played as a half note, for example—while others may be played more quickly than written, such as a half note played as a quarter note.

Phrase 1

There are several accepted rules here. The first thing is, if the melody of the tune that we're playing is on the top strings—the B or E string—whatever solo fill that you're going to play should start from the low strings and move up toward the melody. I'm sure you've heard many musicians play a line and then play some kind of lick, and the last note of that lick is the very first note of the melody that they would then continue with.

So here's how it works: We have a melody to a song and we play that melody. When the melody comes to rest, or where there is a whole note or a half note or some other resting point, we play some kind of lick that fits the chord of the moment.

Phrase 1 is played over an implied Am7 chord, so the scales that I can choose from to fill between melody phrases include A harmonic minor, A melodic minor, A minor pentatonic, A Dorian, A Phrygian—there are a lot of scales I can choose from. In this example, I use A harmonic minor.

Phrase 1

Practice Point 1: I play the first three notes of my melody on the top two strings: E, B, E. The last note brings us to a natural resting point.

Practice Point 2: I begin my solo fill. I start on the low strings, and move up towards the first note of the melody (D) that I'm going to continue with. I use A harmonic minor here, with a chromatic slide up to that final note. Actually, D is both the final note of my fill and the beginning of the next fragment of my melody.

Phrase 2

In Phrase 2, I return to the melody. Then, when it comes to rest again, I insert a solo fill over an implied A7 chord.

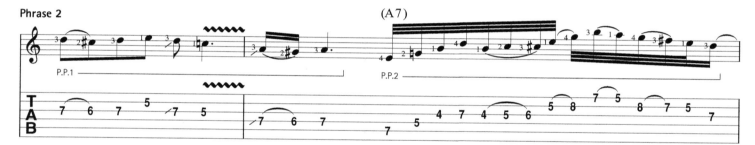

Practice Point 1: I continue with my melody.

Practice Point 2: Now, for my fill: Again, I start low and aim high towards the first note of the next melodic fragment, another D note.

Phrase 3

In Phrase 3, the melody continues over an implied Dm7 chord. I let this phrase breathe a little.

Phrase 4

We don't always have to start our fill at the opposite end. In this phrase, I start my fill in the same register as my melody, then work my way up, and eventually come back down again to the first note of the next melodic fragment.

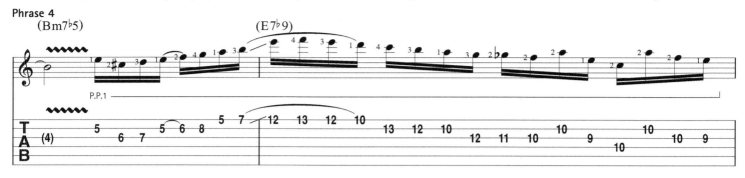

Practice Point 1: My melody has come to rest again, on the note B. I play a fill that implies the turnaround Bm7♭5 and E7♭9, which leads back into an Am chord in the next phrase.

Phrase 5

Phrase 5 marks the return of our first melodic idea over an implied Am chord. I add another fill—this one going from high to low. This is the last fill before setting up the actual body of the song.

Practice Point 1: This fill is a favorite lick based on the A minor pentatonic scale.

Creating Interest for the Listener

Adding fills to a melody like this is one way of creating interest for the listener (and for yourself!). There are other ways to approach this type of introduction:

- You don't have to play only single-note melodies; you could play chords, too. For example, you could play a melodic fragment, harmonize the last note with a chord, and then go into your fill.

- Joe Pass does another thing. Sometimes, he harmonizes his melody, but then when he plays his fill, instead of working towards his next melody note, he'll work towards the root of the chord that's harmonizing his next melody note. (You can utilize a similar approach when playing "chords only" for an introduction, adding fills between your chords and leading from the root of one chord to the root of the next chord.)

- You don't have to play your melody on the upper strings; you could play it on the lower strings instead. Then, you'd begin your fills from the top strings and work your way back down to the next melody note.

- You don't have to restrict your melody to just one register. You could start a tune in one octave, then lower it down to another octave. This can be particularly effective when a melodic idea is repeated—like, in this tune, at the return of the first melodic idea over Am.

- You could also choose an arpeggio, another type of scale, or a different pattern altogether for your fills.

So you can see how exciting these ideas can become.

Phrase 6

After the melody has been played out of tempo in an introduction like this, the player will start to use different little motives—maybe only two or three notes—to establish the tempo of the tune.

Practice Point 1: I'm getting ready to set up a groove.

Practice Point 2: Now I start playing in tempo.

Phrase 7

Phrase 7 is the vamp with which I set up the main melody of the song and bring in the other musicians. After my rubato solo introduction, this vamp allows the drummer to find his time and the bass player to join in as well.

Practice Point 1: I play this simple two-measure phrase three times, at whatever tempo I select. If I want, to signal the start of the tune that follows, I could throw in a ii-V progression right before heading into the tune itself.

The Tune

The tune that I solo over (following my introduction) is basically a 16-bar form in Am. It could also be analyzed as two eight-bar sections, each one beginning on the tonic chord. Harmonically, the progression relies on the i, iv, and V chords (Am7, Dm7, E7#9), with a turnaround (Cmaj7–Fmaj–Bm7♭5–E7♭9) that briefly hints at the relative major key, C.

I solo once through this 16-bar form—I'll let you analyze my solo. You can also practice my licks with the "rhythm only" track at the end of the chapter. Then I let the piano take a solo. When the band reaches the turnaround again, the tempo slows down, coming to rest on the V chord, E7♭9.

The Ending

While the band holds the E7♭9 chord—a point of high tension, musically speaking—the guitar plays a rubato solo ending similar to the introduction. This makes the most of the moment, postponing the inevitable resolution (and thereby increasing the tension) as well as bringing things full circle, for a satisfying conclusion.

Endings such as this are real "show-off" points. I speed things up considerably here, playing some very fast, fluid passages. The fact that the note values fluctuate considerably here is not important; in fact, it's really only of concern in regards to the music transcription. The important thing is that I'm playing *rubato*—simply by feel, without regard for time or tempo.

When the band finally reaches the last i chord, Am7, I wrap up the song with a fast, free-form flourish, capped off by a lick played first in one octave, then an octave lower.

Walking Bass Lines

Although it's not in my solo, another aspect of virtuoso guitar that I'd like to explain is walking bass lines. I'm sure you've heard Joe Pass and other players use this. It's a very simple technique, really; it sounds harder than it actually is.

A walking bass line is one of the jazz bassist's signature tools. It's a bass line that consists primarily of quarter notes, outlining the chord changes by means of important chord tones—like the root and 5th—interspersed with chromatic approaches. The continuous flow of quarter notes keeps time and establishes a sense of forward momentum, much like walking.

When a solo guitarist plays walking bass lines interspersed with chords, it creates a very powerful illusion of two instruments playing at once—guitar and bass. This makes it an attention-getting technique. It's also great for creating contrast in a solo; listeners really notice it.

We'll try this technique using a I–VI–ii–V chord progression: Cmaj7–A13–Dm7–G13

When Chords Change Every Two Beats

Let's start with chords occurring every two beats, like this.

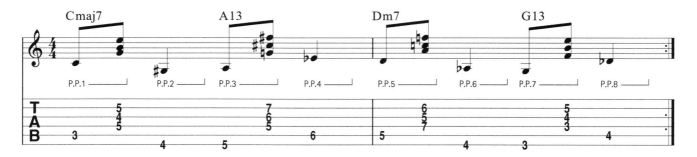

Practice Point 1: Place your fingers on the C chord. On beat 1, play the bass note, C, the root of the chord. Then on the "and" of the beat, play the rest of the chord. So in the time of one beat, we play "bass note, chord." Let the bass note and the chord ring together.

Practice Point 2: Now we have one more beat to play with. On beat 2, we're going to half-step approach the root of the next chord, A13. We can do this from a half step above or below. I chose to approach from below. So on beat 2, play a G# bass note.

Practice Point 3: Now for the A13, we'll play the root followed by the chord, just as before. Hit an A bass note on beat 3, followed by the rest of the chord on the "and."

Practice Point 4: The next chord we're going to is Dm7, so let's half-step approach it, this time from above. So on beat 4, play an E♭ bass note.

Practice Point 5: For Dm7, play a D bass note on beat 1, followed by the rest of the chord on the "and."

Practice Point 6: The next chord we're going to is G13, so let's half-step approach it from above. So on beat 2, we'll play an A♭ bass note.

Practice Point 7: For G13, play a G bass note, followed by the rest of the chord on the "and."

Practice Point 8: We're going back to the Cmaj7 chord, so we'll half-step approach it, from above. So on beat 4, play a D♭ bass note.

And that's it; we've just created a walking bass line—or the illusion of one—just by using chord shapes we already know. Notice that each chord is always played on the "and" of the beat. For our bass line, we use the root of each chord and the notes a half step above or below.

Incidentally, you don't have to play only quarter notes in the bass. Especially if the tempo is a little slower, feel free to add some eighth notes to fill out your line, like this.

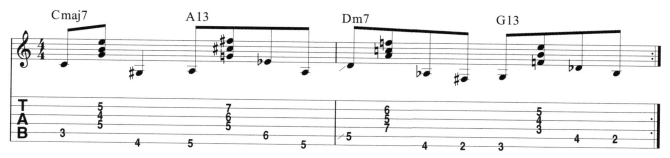

When Chords Last Four Beats or More

Now what if a chord lasts four beats, or eight beats, or thirty beats? Then we need to come up with a slightly different approach.

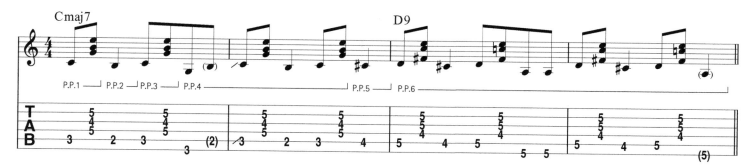

Practice Point 1: Hit the bass note C on beat 1, followed by the rest of the chord on the "and" of the beat.

Practice Point 2: On beat 2, go a half step lower and play a B♮.

Practice Point 3: Go back to the chord and play the bass note C, followed by the rest of the chord.

Practice Point 4: Play the 5th of the chord. (The B note is an optional approach note.)

So now we have a walking bass line that lasts four beats. And we could repeat this indefinitely, for as long as we needed to vamp on this one chord. But what if we need to move on to another chord? Then we need to go back to our half-step approach method.

Practice Point 5: In anticipation of the next chord, D9, I alter my bass line to play a C#, a half step below the root of that chord.

Practice Point 6: I play a similar four-beat walking bass pattern over the D9 chord.

Notice again, the chord is always on the "and" of the beat, and our walking bass line consists of roots or 5ths and the notes a half step above or below. Once you get comfortable with this, it can be sped up and becomes a very powerful tool.

Other Ideas

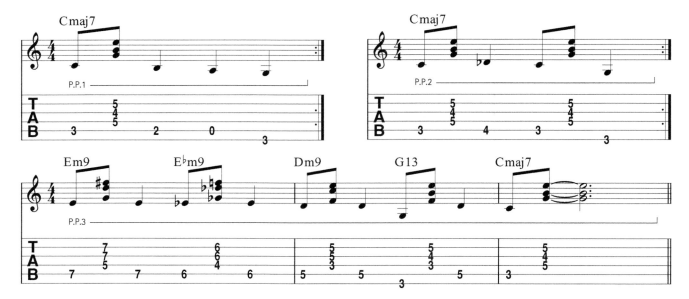

Practice Point 1: If a chord lasts for four beats or more, another option we have is to play the chord only once and use a short descending bass line like this.

Practice Point 2: Or we could play a half step higher than the root. Regardless, we're pivoting around the root.

Practice Point 3: We don't always have to change our bass note when playing over a chord. We could play "bass note, chord, bass note," using the root both times. This is especially effective on a chromatic progression like this, where there's already a strong linear momentum.

Final Word

The role models for virtuoso guitar playing—Joe Pass and Barney Kessel—provide countless hours of inspiration with their solo recordings. In particular you should check out the four-CD series by Joe Pass titled, appropriately enough, *Virtuoso.* I hope this chapter and this entire book have brought new joy to your playing. Good luck and have fun.

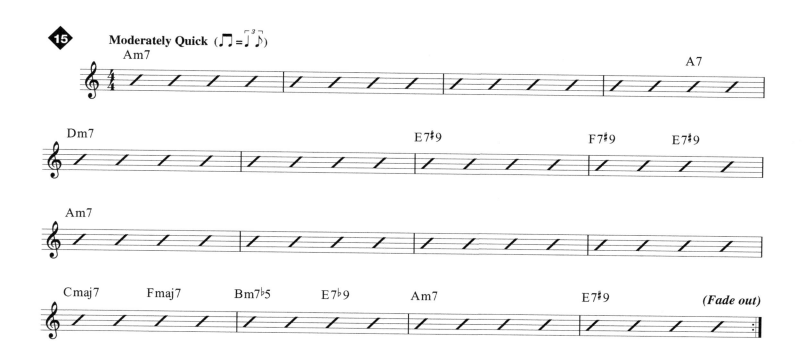

Guitar Notation Legend

Guitar Music can be notated three different ways: on a *musical staff*, in *tablature*, and in *rhythm slashes*.

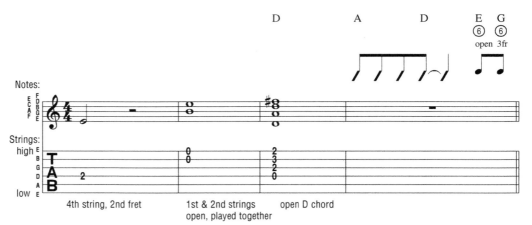

RHYTHM SLASHES are written above the staff. Strum chords in the rhythm indicated. Use the chord diagrams found at the top of the first page of the transcription for the appropriate chord voicings. Round noteheads indicate single notes.

THE MUSICAL STAFF shows pitches and rhythms and is divided by bar lines into measures. Pitches are named after the first seven letters of the alphabet.

TABLATURE graphically represents the guitar fingerboard. Each horizontal line represents a a string, and each number represents a fret.

4th string, 2nd fret

1st & 2nd strings open, played together

open D chord

Definitions for Special Guitar Notation

HALF-STEP BEND: Strike the note and bend up 1/2 step.

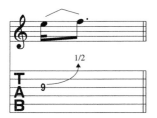

WHOLE-STEP BEND: Strike the note and bend up one step.

GRACE NOTE BEND: Strike the note and immediately bend up as indicated.

SLIGHT (MICROTONE) BEND: Strike the note and bend up 1/4 step.

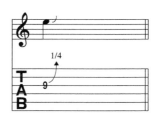

BEND AND RELEASE: Strike the note and bend up as indicated, then release back to the original note. Only the first note is struck.

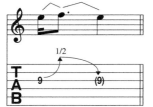

PRE-BEND: Bend the note as indicated, then strike it.

PRE-BEND AND RELEASE: Bend the note as indicated. Strike it and release the bend back to the original note.

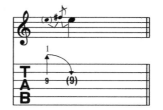

UNISON BEND: Strike the two notes simultaneously and bend the lower note up to the pitch of the higher.

VIBRATO: The string is vibrated by rapidly bending and releasing the note with the fretting hand.

WIDE VIBRATO: The pitch is varied to a greater degree by vibrating with the fretting hand.

HAMMER-ON: Strike the first (lower) note with one finger, then sound the higher note (on the same string) with another finger by fretting it without picking.

PULL-OFF: Place both fingers on the notes to be sounded. Strike the first note and without picking, pull the finger off to sound the second (lower) note.

LEGATO SLIDE: Strike the first note and then slide the same fret-hand finger up or down to the second note. The second note is not struck.

SHIFT SLIDE: Same as legato slide, except the second note is struck.

TRILL: Very rapidly alternate between the notes indicated by continuously hammering on and pulling off.

TAPPING: Hammer ("tap") the fret indicated with the pick-hand index or middle finger and pull off to the note fretted by the fret hand.

NATURAL HARMONIC: Strike the note while the fret-hand lightly touches the string directly over the fret indicated.

Harm.

PINCH HARMONIC: The note is fretted normally and a harmonic is produced by adding the edge of the thumb or the tip of the index finger of the pick hand to the normal pick attack.

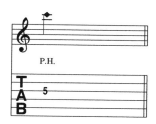

P.H.

HARP HARMONIC: The note is fretted normally and a harmonic is produced by gently resting the pick hand's index finger directly above the indicated fret (in parentheses) while the pick hand's thumb or pick assists by plucking the appropriate string.

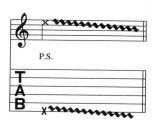

H.H.

PICK SCRAPE: The edge of the pick is rubbed down (or up) the string, producing a scratchy sound.

P.S.

MUFFLED STRINGS: A percussive sound is produced by laying the fret hand across the string(s) without depressing, and striking them with the pick hand.

PALM MUTING: The note is partially muted by the pick hand lightly touching the string(s) just before the bridge.

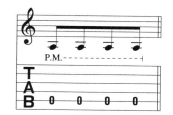

P.M.

RAKE: Drag the pick across the strings indicated with a single motion.

rake

TREMOLO PICKING: The note is picked as rapidly and continuously as possible.

ARPEGGIATE: Play the notes of the chord indicated by quickly rolling them from bottom to top.

VIBRATO BAR DIVE AND RETURN: The pitch of the note or chord is dropped a specified number of steps (in rhythm) then returned to the original pitch.

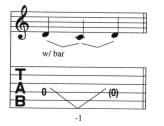

w/ bar

VIBRATO BAR SCOOP: Depress the bar just before striking the note, then quickly release the bar.

w/ bar

VIBRATO BAR DIP: Strike the note and then immediately drop a specified number of steps, then release back to the original pitch.

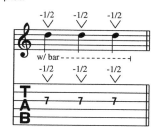

w/ bar

Additional Musical Definitions

(accent)	• Accentuate note (play it louder)	
(accent)	• Accentuate note with great intensity	
(staccato)	• Play the note short	
	• Downstroke	
	• Upstroke	

D.S. al Coda • Go back to the sign ( ), then play until the measure marked "*To Coda*," then skip to the section labelled "**Coda**."

D.C. al Fine • Go back to the beginning of the song and play until the measure marked "*Fine*" (end).

Rhy. Fig. • Label used to recall a recurring accompaniment pattern (usually chordal).

Riff • Label used to recall composed, melodic lines (usually single notes) which recur.

Fill • Label used to identify a brief melodic figure which is to be inserted into the arrangement.

Rhy. Fill • A chordal version of a Fill.

tacet • Instrument is silent (drops out).

• Repeat measures between signs.

• When a repeated section has different endings, play the first ending only the first time and the second ending only the second time.

NOTE: Tablature numbers in parentheses mean:
1. The note is being sustained over a system (note in standard notation is tied), or
2. The note is sustained, but a new articulation (such as a hammer-on, pull-off, slide or vibrato begins), or
3. The note is a barely audible "ghost" note (note in standard notation is also in parentheses).

IMPROVE YOUR IMPROV

AND OTHER JAZZ TECHNIQUES WITH BOOKS FROM HAL LEONARD

JAZZ GUITAR
HAL LEONARD GUITAR METHOD
by Jeff Schroedl

The Hal Leonard Jazz Guitar Method is your complete guide to learning jazz guitar. This book uses real jazz songs to teach the basics of accompanying and improvising jazz guitar in the style of Wes Montgomery, Joe Pass, Tal Farlow, Charlie Christian, Pat Martino, Barney Kessel, Jim Hall, and many others.
00695359 Book/Online Audio $22.99

AMAZING PHRASING
50 WAYS TO IMPROVE YOUR
IMPROVISATIONAL SKILLS • *by Tom Kolb*

This book explores all the main components necessary for crafting well-balanced rhythmic and melodic phrases. It also explains how these phrases are put together to form cohesive solos. Many styles are covered – rock, blues, jazz, fusion, country, Latin, funk and more – and all of the concepts are backed up with musical examples.
00695583 Book/Online Audio $22.99

BEST OF JAZZ GUITAR
by Wolf Marshall • Signature Licks

In this book/audio pack, Wolf Marshall provides a hands-on analysis of 10 of the most frequently played tunes in the jazz genre, as played by the leading guitarists of all time. Each selection includes technical analysis and performance notes, biographical sketches, and authentic matching audio with backing tracks.
00695586 Book/Online Audio $29.99

CHORD-MELODY
PHRASES FOR GUITAR
by Ron Eschete • REH ProLessons Series

Expand your chord-melody chops with these outstanding jazz phrases! This book covers: chord substitutions, chromatic movements, contrary motion, pedal tones, inner-voice movements, reharmonization techniques, and much more. Includes standard notation and tab, and online audio.
00695628 Book/Online Audio $17.99

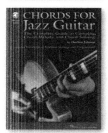

CHORDS FOR JAZZ GUITAR
THE COMPLETE GUIDE TO COMPING,
CHORD MELODY AND CHORD SOLOING • *by Charlton Johnson*

This book/audio pack will teach you how to play jazz chords all over the fretboard in a variety of styles and progressions. It covers: voicings, progressions, jazz chord theory, comping, chord melody, chord soloing, voice leading and many more topics. The audio offers 98 full-band demo tracks. No tablature.
00695706 Book/Online Audio $19.99

FRETBOARD ROADMAPS –
JAZZ GUITAR
THE ESSENTIAL GUITAR PATTERNS
THAT ALL THE PROS KNOW AND USE • *by Fred Sokolow*

This book will get guitarists playing lead & rhythm anywhere on the fretboard, in any key! It teaches a variety of lead guitar styles using moveable patterns, double-note licks, sliding pentatonics and more, through easy-to-follow diagrams and instructions. The online audio includes 54 full-demo tracks.
00695354 Book/Online Audio $17.99

JAZZ IMPROVISATION FOR GUITAR
by Les Wise • REH ProLessons Series

This book/audio will allow you to make the transition from playing disjointed scales and arpeggios to playing melodic jazz solos that maintain continuity and interest for the listener. Topics covered include: tension and resolution, major scale, melodic minor scale, and harmonic minor scale patterns, common licks and substitution techniques, creating altered tension, and more! Features standard notation and tab, and online audio.
00695657 Book/Online Audio $19.99

JAZZ RHYTHM GUITAR
THE COMPLETE GUIDE
by Jack Grassel

This book/audio pack will help rhythm guitarists better understand: chord symbols and voicings, comping styles and patterns, equipment, accessories and set-up, the fingerboard, chord theory, and much more. The accompanying online audio includes 74 full-band tracks.
00695654 Book/Online Audio $24.99

JAZZ SOLOS FOR GUITAR
LEAD GUITAR IN THE STYLES OF TAL FARLOW,
BARNEY KESSEL, WES MONTGOMERY, JOE PASS, JOHNNY SMITH
by Les Wise

Examine the solo concepts of the masters with this book including phrase-by-phrase performance notes, tips on arpeggio substitution, scale substitution, tension and resolution, jazz-blues, chord soloing, and more. The audio includes full demonstration and rhythm-only tracks.
00695447 Book/Online Audio $19.99

100 JAZZ LESSONS
Guitar Lesson Goldmine Series
by John Heussenstamm and Paul Silbergleit

Featuring 100 individual modules covering a giant array of topics, each lesson includes detailed instruction with playing examples presented in standard notation and tablature. You'll also get extremely useful tips, scale diagrams, and more to reinforce your learning experience, plus audio featuring performance demos of all the examples in the book!
00696454 Book/Online Audio $24.99

101 MUST-KNOW JAZZ LICKS
A QUICK, EASY REFERENCE GUIDE
FOR ALL GUITARISTS • *by Wolf Marshall*

Here are 101 definitive licks, plus demonstration audio, from every major jazz guitar style, neatly organized into easy-to-use categories. They're all here: swing and pre-bop, bebop, post-bop modern jazz, hard bop and cool jazz, modal jazz, soul jazz and postmodern jazz. Includes an introduction, tips, and a list of suggested recordings.
00695433 Book/Online Audio $19.99

SWING AND BIG BAND GUITAR
FOUR-TO-THE-BAR COMPING IN THE STYLE OF
FREDDIE GREEN • *by Charlton Johnson*

This unique package teaches the essentials of swing and big band styles, including chord voicings, inversions, substitutions; time and groove, reading charts, chord reduction, and expansion; sample songs, patterns, progressions, and exercises; chord reference library; and online audio with over 50 full-demo examples. Uses chord grids – no tablature.
00695147 Book/Online Audio $22.99

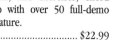

HAL•LEONARD®
Visit Hal Leonard Online at **www.halleonard.com**

*Prices, contents and availability
subject to change without notice.*

PLAY THE CLASSICS

JAZZ FOLIOS FOR GUITARISTS

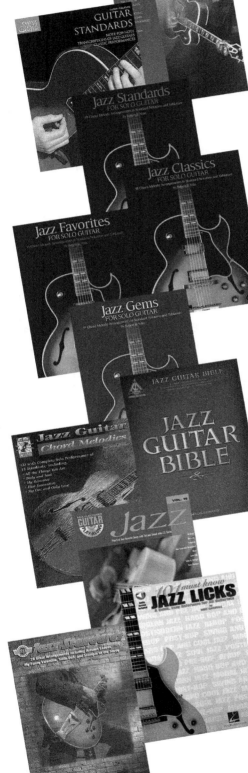

BEST OF JAZZ GUITAR
by Wolf Marshall • Signature Licks

In this book/audio pack, Wolf Marshall provides a hands-on analysis of 10 of the most frequently played tunes in the jazz genre, as played by the leading guitarists of all time. Features: All the Things You Are • How Insensitive • I'll Remember April • So What • Yesterdays • and more.
00695586 Book/Online Audio................................ $29.99

GUITAR STANDARDS
Classic Jazz Masters Series

16 classic jazz guitar performances transcribed note for note with tablature: All of You (Kenny Burrell) • Easter Parade (Herb Ellis) • I'll Remember April (Grant Green) • Lover Man (Django Reinhardt) • Song for My Father (George Benson) • The Way You Look Tonight (Wes Montgomery) • and more. Includes a discography.
00699143 Guitar Transcriptions $14.95

JAZZ CLASSICS FOR SOLO GUITAR
arranged by Robert B. Yelin

This collection includes excellent chord melody arrangements in standard notation and tablature for 35 all-time jazz favorites: April in Paris • Cry Me a River • Day by Day • God Bless' the Child • It Might as Well Be Spring • Lover • My Romance • Nuages • Satin Doll • Tenderly • Unchained Melody • Wave • and more!
00699279 Solo Guitar $19.99

JAZZ FAVORITES FOR SOLO GUITAR
arranged by Robert B. Yelin

This fantastic 35-song collection includes lush chord melody arrangements in standard notation and tab: Autumn in New York • Call Me Irresponsible • How Deep Is the Ocean • I Could Write a Book • The Lady Is a Tramp • Mood Indigo • Polka Dots and Moonbeams • Solitude • Take the "A" Train • Where or When • more.
00699278 Solo Guitar $19.99

JAZZ GEMS FOR SOLO GUITAR
arranged by Robert B. Yelin

35 great solo arrangements of jazz classics, including: After You've Gone • Alice in Wonderland • The Christmas Song • Four • Meditation • Stompin' at the Savoy • Sweet and Lovely • Waltz for Debby • Yardbird Suite • You'll Never Walk Alone • You've Changed • and more.
00699617 Solo Guitar $19.99

JAZZ GUITAR BIBLE

The one book that has all of the jazz guitar classics transcribed note-for-note, with standard notation and tablature. Includes over 30 songs: Body and Soul • Girl Talk • I'll Remember April • In a Sentimental Mood • My Funny Valentine • Nuages • Satin Doll • So What • Stardust • Take Five • Tangerine • Yardbird Suite • and more.
00690466 Guitar Recorded Versions $27.99

JAZZ GUITAR CHORD MELODIES
arranged & performed by Dan Towey

This book/CD pack includes complete solo performances of 12 standards, including: All the Things You Are • Body and Soul • My Romance • How Insensitive • My One and Only Love • and more. The arrangements are performance level and range in difficulty from intermediate to advanced.
00698988 Book/CD Pack.. $19.95

JAZZ GUITAR PLAY-ALONG
Guitar Play-Along Volume 16

With this book/audio pack, all you have to do is follow the tab, listen to the online audio to hear how the guitar should sound, and then play along using the separate backing tracks. 8 songs: All Blues • Bluesette • Footprints • How Insensitive (Insensatez) • Misty • Satin Doll • Stella by Starlight • Tenor Madness.
00699584 Book/Online Audio.............................. $16.99

JAZZ STANDARDS FOR FINGERSTYLE GUITAR

20 songs, including: All the Things You Are • Autumn Leaves • Bluesette • Body and Soul • Fly Me to the Moon • The Girl from Ipanema • How Insensitive • I've Grown Accustomed to Her Face • My Funny Valentine • Satin Doll • Stompin' at the Savoy • and more.
00699029 Fingerstyle Guitar $17.99

JAZZ STANDARDS FOR SOLO GUITAR
arranged by Robert B. Yelin

35 chord melody guitar arrangements, including: Ain't Misbehavin' • Autumn Leaves • Bewitched • Cherokee • Darn That Dream • Girl Talk • I've Got You Under My Skin • Lullaby of Birdland • My Funny Valentine • A Nightingale Sang in Berkeley Square • Stella by Starlight • The Very Thought of You • and more.
00699277 Solo Guitar $19.99

101 MUST-KNOW JAZZ LICKS
by Wolf Marshall

Add a jazz feel and flavor to your playing! 101 definitive licks, plus demonstration audio, from every major jazz guitar style, neatly organized into easy-to-use categories. They're all here: swing and pre-bop, bebop, post-bop modern jazz, hard bop and cool jazz, modal jazz, soul jazz and postmodern jazz.
00695433 Book/Online Audio.............................. $19.99

HAL•LEONARD®

Visit Hal Leonard Online at **www.halleonard.com**

Prices, contents and availability subject to change without notice.

GUITAR *signature licks*®

Signature Licks book/audio packs provide a step-by-step breakdown of "right from the record" riffs, licks, and solos so you can jam along with your favorite bands. They contain performance notes and an overview of each artist's or group's style, with note-for-note transcriptions in notes and tab. The online audio tracks feature full-band demos at both normal and slow speeds.

AC/DC
14041352.....................$24.99

AEROSMITH 1973-1979
00695106.....................$24.99

AEROSMITH 1979-1998
00695219..................... $22.95

DUANE ALLMAN
00696042.....................$24.99

BEST OF CHET ATKINS
00695752.....................$24.99

AVENGED SEVENFOLD
00696473.....................$24.99

THE BEATLES
00298845.....................$24.99

BEST OF THE BEATLES FOR ACOUSTIC GUITAR
00695453.....................$24.99

THE BEATLES HITS
00695049.....................$24.95

JEFF BECK
00696427.....................$24.99

BEST OF GEORGE BENSON
00695418..................... $22.99

BEST OF BLACK SABBATH
00695249.....................$24.99

BLUES BREAKERS WITH JOHN MAYALL & ERIC CLAPTON
00696374.....................$24.99

BON JOVI
00696380..................... $22.99

ROY BUCHANAN
00696654..................... $22.99

KENNY BURRELL
00695830.....................$27.99

BEST OF CHARLIE CHRISTIAN
00695584.....................$24.99

BEST OF ERIC CLAPTON
00695038.....................$24.99

ERIC CLAPTON – FROM THE ALBUM UNPLUGGED
00695250.....................$24.99

BEST OF CREAM
00695251 ....$24.99

THE DOORS
00695373 .... $22.95

DEEP PURPLE – GREATEST HITS
00695625.....................$24.99

DREAM THEATER
00111943.....................$24.99

TOMMY EMMANUEL
00696409.....................$22.99

ESSENTIAL JAZZ GUITAR
00695875.....................$19.99

FLEETWOOD MAC
00696416 ....$22.99

ROBBEN FORD
00695903 ....$22.95

BEST OF GRANT GREEN
00695747 ....$24.99

PETER GREEN
00145386.....................$24.99

BEST OF GUNS N' ROSES
00695183.....................$24.99

THE BEST OF BUDDY GUY
00695186 ....$22.99

JIM HALL
00695848 ....$29.99

JIMI HENDRIX
00696560.....................$24.99

JIMI HENDRIX – VOLUME 2
00695835 ....$24.99

JOHN LEE HOOKER
00695894.....................$24.99

BEST OF JAZZ GUITAR
00695586.....................$29.99

ERIC JOHNSON
00699317.....................$24.99

ROBERT JOHNSON
00695264.....................$24.99

BARNEY KESSEL
00696009.....................$24.99

THE ESSENTIAL ALBERT KING
00695713.....................$24.99

B.B. KING – BLUES LEGEND
00696039 ....$22.99

B.B. KING – THE DEFINITIVE COLLECTION
00695635 .... $22.99

MARK KNOPFLER
00695178.....................$24.99

LYNYRD SKYNYRD
00695872.....................$24.99

THE BEST OF YNGWIE MALMSTEEN
00695669.....................$24.99

BEST OF PAT MARTINO
00695632.....................$24.99

MEGADETH
00696421.....................$22.99

WES MONTGOMERY
00695387.....................$24.99

BEST OF NIRVANA
00695483.....................$24.95

VERY BEST OF OZZY OSBOURNE
00695431.....................$22.99

BRAD PAISLEY
00696379.....................$22.99

BEST OF JOE PASS
00695730.....................$24.99

TOM PETTY
00696021.....................$24.99

PINK FLOYD
00103659.....................$27.99

THE GUITARS OF ELVIS
00174800.....................$22.99

BEST OF QUEEN
00695097.....................$24.99

RADIOHEAD
00109304.....................$24.99

BEST OF RAGE AGAINST THE MACHINE
00695480.....................$24.99

JERRY REED
00118236 ....$22.99

BEST OF DJANGO REINHARDT
00695660.....................$27.99

BEST OF ROCK 'N' ROLL GUITAR
00695559.....................$24.99

BEST OF ROCKABILLY GUITAR
00695785.....................$22.99

BEST OF CARLOS SANTANA
00174664 ....$22.99

BEST OF JOE SATRIANI
00695216 ....$24.99

SLASH
00696576.....................$22.99

SLAYER
00121281.....................$22.99

BEST OF SOUTHERN ROCK
00695560.....................$19.95

STEELY DAN
00696015.....................$22.99

MIKE STERN
00695800.....................$27.99

BEST OF SURF GUITAR
00695822.....................$22.99

STEVE VAI
00673247.....................$24.99

STEVE VAI – ALIEN LOVE SECRETS: THE NAKED VAMPS
00695223.....................$27.99

STEVE VAI – FIRE GARDEN: THE NAKED VAMPS
00695166 ....$22.95

STEVE VAI – THE ULTRA ZONE: NAKED VAMPS
00695684.....................$22.95

VAN HALEN
00110227.....................$27.99

THE GUITAR STYLE OF STEVIE RAY VAUGHAN
00695155.....................$24.95

BEST OF THE VENTURES
00695772.....................$24.99

THE WHO – 2ND ED.
00695561 ....$22.95

JOHNNY WINTER
00695951 ....$24.99

YES
00113120.....................$24.99

NEIL YOUNG – GREATEST HITS
00695988.....................$24.99

BEST OF ZZ TOP
00695738.....................$24.99

HAL•LEONARD®

www.halleonard.com

COMPLETE DESCRIPTIONS AND SONGLISTS ONLINE!

Prices, contents and availability subject to change without notice.

0622
305